TWICKENHAM

A HISTORY OF THE
CATHEDRAL OF RUGBY

To Sue, who suffers me so well.

TWICKENHAM

A HISTORY OF THE CATHEDRAL OF RUGBY

Ed Harris

SPORTS BOOKS

Published in Great Britain by
SportsBooks Limited
PO Box 422
Cheltenham
GL50 2YN

© Ed Harris 2005
First Published September 2005

Front cover designed by Kath Northam.

Front cover photograph: EMPICS
Back cover: Rugby Football Union

A catalogue record for this book is available from
the British Library.
ISBN 1 899807 29 2

Printed and bound in England by Creative Print and
Design Ltd, Wales.

INTRODUCTION

During the 19th century, as British industries such as shipping and mining began a slow decline, there was created a need to look for other economic activities such as those to be found within the goods and services sectors. Included in this was the concept of recreation as a sound social, as well as economic, proposition. As more and more people began to shift from the land into the towns and cities, time was no longer governed by seasonal variations but by the machine and the factory clock. Increasing leisure activities became more important in the lives of people from all classes and all walks of life, and no more so than in sport.

Not one hundred and fifty years have passed since football shifted from open fields, sometimes with the luxury of a wooden grandstand, into purpose-built grounds. Now, these key features of local, national and international identity have grown beyond recognition to include portable pitches and retractable roofs. But while these dramatic additions to the local landscape can be just as fascinating as any great house, church or cathedral, complete with as much scheming, plotting and political intrigue, they are rarely celebrated. Instead, the football stadium tends to sit with the gasometer or the power station in the affections of the historian and tourist guidebooks.

What hard history has been written about Twickenham Rugby Ground is mostly passed down from one man. Since O L Owen wrote *The History of the Rugby Football Union* in the 1950s, nothing since has tested or questioned his partial and idealised perspective, founded as it was on a genuine love of the game and respect for the values imbued in the Rugby Football Union. As effectively the public relations man for what he described as an 'understandably shy organisation', Owen glossed over many of the details as to exactly how such a pitiable site for the home of England Rugby came to be selected.

Twickenham Rugby Ground epitomises the plight of the football stadium. While millions travel miles to get inside them, no one wants one as a neighbour. Despite the fact that more people file through their turnstiles on a single day than cross the threshold of many a museum in an entire year, football grounds enjoy prominence mostly as a nuisance. Just as the Great Wall of China is the most visible man-made structure from outer space, so 'The Cathedral of Rugby' at Twickenham blights Arcadia on Thames from Richmond Hill.

Against the odds, the stadium did bring success to an ailing English national game, but it also began a journey that was long and unnecessarily hard. Had the original scheme to secure a ground been sound then Stamford Bridge would today be the home of England Rugby, and had the entrepreneurial wheels spun more efficiently, then for Twickenham we might even read Wembley. Instead, there was secured an affordable though by no means popular choice of site, but one that set the tone for the England game. A century later and the story of Twickenham Rugby Ground is the story of England Rugby.

Ed Harris

CONTENTS

Acknowledgements

My thanks and appreciation in particular to Dr Chris French of Kingston University for his guidance, skill and patience throughout the development of this eventual publication, and to Keith Greaves, Robert Gant and Peter Tilley, and to all of those associated with the Kingston University Masters Degree in Local History where the process began. My thanks also to Jane Baxter and Christine Turfitt at the Richmond upon Thames Local Studies Collection; to Jed Smith, Rex King, John Clark and Ross Hamilton at the Rugby Football Union for their unstinting help and assistance throughout the research process. Thanks, as well, to staff at the Public Record Office, The British Newspaper Library, National Army Museum, Scottish Rugby Union, National Register of Archives (Scotland), Westminster City Archive, London Metropolitan Archive, Essex Record Office, Stratford Library, Hammersmith and Fulham Archive and the General Register Office. Much gratitude, too, for the generous hospitality and assistance afforded by George Kirk of Edwin Coe Solicitors, Lincoln's Inn. Also to the doyen of sports ground history, Simon Inglis, for his sound advice, and to the many local residents who kindly gave of their time to record their memories; especially 'Miss Christie' for her memories of early 20th century Twickenham spectatorship; Harold Clark and Alf Wright for use of their memoirs, and to Les Felsham (Kneller Hall) for his introduction to Billy and Allen Williams. My sincerest apologies go to anyone missing from this list.

Ed Harris

TWICKENHAM TIMELINE

1905   The arrival of the original All Blacks. England on a massive losing streak. RFU Treasurer, William Cail, takes action.

1906   Billy Williams scouts the London area for an England home ground.

1907   Cail submits his proposal to the RFU. A plot of 8.9 acres of land 'in the middle of nowhere' is purchased.
       Harlequins sign a lease as the new ground's tenants.

1908   Groundsman's Cottage is built.
       Pitch raised as a defence against flooding.

1909   A and B stands built and South Terrace started.
       Saturday 2nd October. Opening Day. The new ground's tenants, Harlequins, beat visitors Richmond 14-10.

1910   Saturday 15th January – the first international. England beat Wales for the first time in 12 years by a goal, a penalty and a try to two tries.
       F E Chapman for England becomes the first player to score a try, convert and kick a penalty in an international at Twickenham.

1912   Access to the ground more of a problem. The London and South West Railway refuse a Halt at Whitton. Twickenham Urban District Council fails to back a tube link from Richmond.

1913   RFU acquires the remaining 1.6 acres conveyed in 1907 – total ground area: 10.5 acres.

1914   Having won the championship, shared it with Ireland in 1912 and twice won the Triple Crown, England wins the Grand Slam.
       War declared with Germany. An instruction is

circulated to players to volunteer to fight for their country.

The rugby game and Twickenham lie dormant.

1919 1st March – play resumes. King George V presents Royal Trophy to New Zealand at Twickenham.

1921 First University Match played at Twickenham.

1923 District councils, transport companies, residents' associations and the Metropolitan Police demand proper transport links.

An alternative site to Twickenham is sought by the RFU.

1924 The first omnibus service serves Twickenham Stadium.

RFU purchases seven acres of land to begin the west car park.

Record crowd of 43,000 attend the Calcutta Cup.

May: William Cail meets with stadium architect Archibald Leitch to agree the building of a North Stand. August: Cail is stood down after 36 years RFU service.

1925 Sell-out for new 10,500 seat North Stand 3rd January; record 60,000 watch New Zealand victory, 11-17, and 'The Brownlie Incident'.

Vanda Lodge demolished.

Rugby Lodge (216 Whitton Road) built for assistant secretary. 'South View' (182 Whitton Road) purchased for the secretary.

1926 (Middlesex) Sevens arrive as the last fixture of the year.

1927 15th January – first live sports outside broadcast by the BBC: England v Wales at Twickenham (England 11 Wales 9).

East Stand 'double-decked' to accommodate 5,000 extra spectators.

1928 Last flooding of the ground.

Sir George Rowland Hill dies. The Rowland Hill

Memorial and Entrance constructed.
England beat Wales 8-3 before a 65,000 crowd at
Twickenham.

1929   Twickenham Borough Sports Day introduced.
1930   First stage of double-decker West Stand begun.
1931   New West Stand completed raising ground capacity
to 74,000.
Six acres purchased, kick-starting the north car park.
Whitton Station built and town developing.
1933   Twickenham Bridge and sections of A316 Great
Chertsey Road begun.
1934   Oakley Lodge (178 Whitton Road) purchased by
RFU and demolished to make way for a new ticket
gate.
1937   A316 Chertsey Road declared Class One Motor
Route.
1939   50th international played at Twickenham: England
(0) v Ireland (5). First special police guard following
IRA bomb threats.
Germany invades Poland. Second World War
begins. All sporting fixtures cancelled. Twickenham
Stadium requisitioned as a civil defence depot and
chemical decontamination centre.
1945   22nd June, first post-war AGM of the RFU.
First post-war game: New Zealand Army Touring
Side (18) v England Fifteen (3).
1946   Services Tournament and Middlesex Sevens return
to Twickenham.
1947   University Match played for the first time on a
Saturday in front of a record 40,000 crowd.
1948   University Match returned to weekday before
another record-breaking 59,400 in attendance.
1950   England beat Wales 11-5 before a 75,532 crowd.
The South Terrace clock tower is demolished and
replaced by the Hermes weathervane.
New Twickenham railway station built.

1951   14th April, Billy Williams dies.
1954   Jehovah's Witnesses' first convention at
        Twickenham.
1955   Number 202, Whitton Road, purchased by the RFU.
1959   Twickenham Jubilee.
1962   Number 176, Whitton Road, purchased by the RFU.
1964   Plans submitted for a South Stand.
        England forces a 5-5 draw with dominant France at
        Twickenham.
        First Clerk of Works drags Twickenham into the
        20th century.
1965   Planning permission for South Stand rejected.
        Parking is a big issue and the view is spoiled from
        Richmond Hill.
        Double-decking the west car park considered.
        Andy Hancock runs his famous 90 metres try to
        deny Scotland their first win at Twickenham since
        1938.
1967   Numbers 180, 208 and 226, Whitton Road
        purchased by the RFU.
1969   Numbers 172, 174 and 220 purchased by the RFU.
        South Stand scheme abandoned due to high
        construction costs.
1970   To save wear on the pitch, pre-international games
        reduced
1971   Rugby Football Union Centenary Year: Greater
        London Council presents RFU with the
        Twickenham Lion.
1974   Safety of Sports Grounds Act will require all stadia
        to obtain a licence. Capacity of the crumbling South
        Terrace reduced to 15,000.
1975   Safety certificate allowing for ground capacity
        below 70,000. Twickenham becomes uneconomic;
        an alternative site is sought.
1979   Planning application for a South Stand submitted
        and agreed in principle.

1980   Low-key corporate hospitality process begins.
       Weathervane and the 'Twickenham Rose' registered
       for marketing purposes.
       South Terrace demolished.
1981   Bare bones of the new South Stand ready in time for
       Calcutta Cup.
1982   Erica Roe becomes Twickenham's most famous
       streaker.
       South Stand Rose Room Banqueting Suite, Museum,
       Shop and 12 Executive Boxes ready in time for the
       first international.
1983   Diamond Vision Screens introduced.
1984   First stadium tour takes place.
1985   230 Whitton Road purchased by the RFU.
       Ground capacity down to 62,000, or one fifth of gate
       revenue.
1989   The Hillsborough tragedy in which 96 spectators
       die gives rise to all-seater stadia.
       Harlequins look to end their 'special relationship' at
       Twickenham.
       Twickenham's bid to host the 1991 World Cup is
       dented by reduced capacity. RFU look to a new
       North Stand but space is limited by allotments and
       parking, now a planning requirement.
       RFU spends £1.5 million to secure allotments land.
       Demolition of the North Stand starts.
       The Groundsman's Cottage is demolished.
1990   New North Stand opens.
       Core objective achieved to raise capacity to 72,000
       for the World Cup.
1991   England loses out to Australia in the World Cup but
       wins the Grand Slam.
       Tesco purchase South Middlesex Hospital site for
       superstore and housing.
       RFU acquire a 99-year lease on Cardinal Vaughn
       Playing Field for parking on match days.

1992 RFU acquire allotments abutting North Stand. East Stand demolished.
1993 New East Stand 'topped out'.
1994 Planning permission submitted for new West Stand; demolition work begins immediately after Middlesex Sevens. 10,000 seats available in time for England v Romania 17th November.
1995 West Stand fully operational 18th November for England v South Africa – the first floodlit game ever at Twickenham – watched by 75,000 spectators. Rugby Union turns professional.
1996 England wins Five Nations Championship. Rowland Hill Memorial with newly gilded Twickenham Lion and bronze statues of players repositioned to form a new entrance from the west car park.
1999 England beats the newcomers Italy, and France and Scotland at Twickenham to win the first Six Nations Grand Slam.
2000 Staging of the Lincoln Financial Group Rugby League World Cup. RFU announces international athletics at Twickenham but its application fails.
2002 New South Stand announced. World record 18 consecutive Tests unbeaten at one ground, 'Fortress Twickenham' becomes part of the rugby vocabulary.
2003 Permission granted for three concerts a year at Twickenham. The Rolling Stones at Twickenham (Sunday 24th August). Mayor of London expresses doubt over South Stand redevelopment. Richmond upon Thames pass redevelopment plans.
2005 South Stand and numbers 170-182, Whitton Road, demolished.

Chapter One

A TALE OF TWO WILLIAMS

All-round good egg, William 'Billy' Williams is traditionally credited as the man of vision who discovered the Twickenham site and who battled against great odds to secure it for the Rugby Football Union, whereas its chief architect, William Cail, has been virtually airbrushed from its history. Billy Williams was little more than Cail's factotum and stooge, who shouldered the derisory mantle of 'Cabbage Patch' used to describe the dubious location set in the flat, featureless wilds of west Middlesex north of Twickenham town. William Cail's prominence in the story of Twickenham Rugby Ground is made all the more remarkable by its absence.

'We glory in the outlawry pronounced on us', wrote an anonymous correspondent to the *Yorkshire Post* in 1895, 'as freeing us from the tyrannical bondage of the English union, and we breathe pure air in being freed from the stifling atmosphere of deceit in which we previously existed.' William Cail was President of the Rugby Football Union at this time and is credited with seeing it through possibly the most traumatic period in its history. After 1895, from a membership of 481 clubs belonging to the Union, that number had fallen to 383. So strong was the feeling that the RFU was prejudiced against the working men of the North that twenty-two Lancashire and Yorkshire clubs resigned to form the rival Northern Union. Thereafter the drift away was steady.

The son of a Tyneside businessman, William Cail was educated in Newcastle and Stuttgart where he studied chemical engineering, before going on to the Sorbonne. Cail's was a typical middle-class background of the 'new gentry'. One of the industrial bourgeoisie, he was later to follow in the footsteps of four previous generations of councillors, three of them aldermen and one a mayor. Outside of business, and second only to his passion for politics, was his enthusiasm for sport, and in particular rugby football.

Cail's first recollection of football was at his grandfather's house in Yorkshire where he spent the summer months. It was there that his father would host an afternoon of entertainments, chief of which was a game of football between the two neighbouring villages played in the old traditional style, but with a degree of respectability that reflected Cail's social origins.

It was as an acclaimed rower and yachtsman that William Cail fully acknowledged the amateur principle in sport. He held the Tyne amateur rowing championship and won more than 50 prizes. However, this was against the backdrop of an uncomfortable reality wherein working-class scullers and rowers dominated both the local and national rowing scene. Amateurs such as Cail simply could not compete with those who rowed for a living. This in turn became a root cause for segregation, wherein the lower orders could not be allowed to beat their betters.

When the Rugby Football Union was formed in 1871, no mention was made in the formulation of its rules of the amateur status of the game. The terms amateur and professional signified the type of man who played the sport. The amateur was a gentleman who played fair and regarded his opponents with respect. The professional was out to win. Standards of play were based upon the experience and high morale of the old boys from the public schools and universities. But this was limited by a reluctance to take the game as seriously as the practical enthusiasts of the north. For the most part, London clubs were severely limited by a lack of players, officials, and suitable grounds. Yorkshire and Lancashire were among the first to take up the Rugby game, to play it hard and organise it well. They were imbued with a doctrine of complete physical fitness and the will to win.

William Cail was instrumental in the formation of Northumberland Rugby Football Union in 1880. It was from there that he became a national union committee member two years later, just as the whole question of professionalism became a national talking point. So much so, that in 1886, the RFU began the process of formal legislation, with Cail as Chairman of the Standing Committee on Professionalism. It was this committee that drafted the new laws which made illegal monetary gain from whatever source or form. Nevertheless, it was William Cail who first embraced the expansion of the Rugby Union game, which at the turn of the last century was increasing the profitability of many clubs. Crowds of 20,000 in the north were not uncommon and the England v Scotland internationals ensured large attendances. Yet, this was anathema to most of the RFU hierarchy who saw in these large and often excitable hordes nothing but 'a nuisance'.

Cail's peers were content to squander the Union's limited resources travelling to and from rented grounds up and down the country, whereas concerns about the lack of logistical and financial control over its game had led the Scottish Rugby Union to search for a ground of its own as early as 1890. In 1897 it purchased land at Inverleith in Edinburgh for £3,800. By 1901 a reporters' box and telephone office was added, and additional land was purchased in 1905. The Irish were settled in Lansdowne Road, and in the same year that the Welsh Rugby Union was formed (1881) the first stand was built at The Cardiff Arms Park boasting 300 seats and costing £50 to erect. Its first, truly 'grand' stand was opened on Boxing Day 1885 and built at a cost of £362. The time, therefore, was over-ripe for England to have a ground of its own. While Cail continued to believe profoundly in the amateur principle, he was committed to moving forward and meeting the challenge of transforming the Rugby Football Union from 'an old-fashioned, almost archaic body' into a 'great modern concern'.

Besides proving to the Northern Union that it meant business, the RFU had also to demonstrate its confidence in its own players, as all the while there was a real danger that the game in the South might waste away. Some grand, expansive gesture on the part of the Union was by now long overdue. The solution, however, was to present something of a conundrum amongst the deeply principled RFU hierarchy.

Cail was just as steeped in the old values as any of his contemporaries. While others wanted to maintain the status quo, he could see in the growing crowds a lucrative, money-spinning potential. Where his worldview collided with his peers was in the belief that the popularisation of the game would prevent keeping the working class where they belonged, in the factories, and yet the big gates signalled the possibility of profiting from the new sport. By 1903, the number of clubs belonging to the RFU was halved and, lacking its northern input, English rugby presented some serious weaknesses. In 1905, a resolution to this dilemma was prompted by a series of events.

Firstly, G Rowland Hill stepped down as the last Honorary Secretary of the RFU after 23 years service. He maintained that his last 10 years in the role was all the more memorable because of his association with William Cail whom he considered to be the RFU's all-important financial adviser. When Rowland Hill was elected President of the RFU he created the first full-time salaried posts in the form of Secretary and Assistant Secretary. In so doing he 'opened the way to modernity' and in turn for Cail the right climate in which to operate.

Secondly was the arrival of the original All Blacks. With their new formation and style of play, the New Zealanders awakened public interest in the game in England. Since the split with the northern clubs, England had not once won the international championship, and in five seasons had been beaten by every one of the home countries.

In order to offer the maximum number of spectators a chance of seeing England play the All Blacks, the RFU had to lease the inhospitable Crystal Palace arena in Sydenham, south London, where some 45,000 spectators – a record crowd for a rugby match in England – watched the visitors thrash the home side five tries to nil.

Ever the businessman, William Cail put this dismal result to one side and looked instead to the record number of spectators and the Union's profit on the fixture of £1,300. The overall cost of hiring grounds for internationals in London was running at around £3,000 and England Rugby was failing. With its own ground, complete with an ample supply of covered seats in permanent stands generating much larger receipts, and with a proper fixture list, turnstiles regulating ticketed entrance and the incorporation of the RFU's offices into the stands saving on London rents, it made sound economic sense for the Rugby Football Union to build a permanent football ground.

Thirdly, controversy was already raging over the legitimacy or otherwise of the New Zealand wing forward Dave Gallaher inserting the ball in the scrummage. In a match against Surrey, the referee, one William 'Billy' Williams, was so incensed, that his handling of the match became a newspaper sensation, provoking headlines such as 'Whistling Fantasia' or 'The Whistle Breaks Down'. The New Zealanders were outraged by the awarding of 14 penalty kicks against them in the first half and two in the second, limiting the tourists' scoring to 11 points when otherwise it would have been a total basting for Surrey. According to former RFU assistant secretary and archivist, Alf Wright, it was at this point that the referee 'probably endeared himself to the Rugby Union, and to its treasurer, William Cail'.

That referee was destined to become synonymous with Twickenham Rugby Ground, not for a dazzling display on the field of play or some amazing contribution to the game, but for finding a former market garden that would become 'Rugby HQ'. A celebrated cricketer, who had appeared as wicketkeeper for Middlesex and toured for England, he played rugby for his college and later Harlequins. Attaching his portrait in the Museum of Rugby at Twickenham, due credit is afforded his discovery of the stadium site and his dogged determination against all odds to secure it. Otherwise, his life and times, like that of

William Cail, has until now occupied minimal space in the annals of Rugby Football Union history.

Billy Williams was something of an enigma, beginning with his date of birth and the age he was when he died. Obituary notices in *The Times* and *Wisden's Directory* variously stated that he was born on 12th April 1860 and that he was 90 years of age when he died on 14th April 1951. Whereas his death certificate gives his age as 90, the census return for 1901 gives his age as 39, in which case he would have been born in 1862. All of this is of minimal interest until attempts are made to trace a particular William Williams amongst the cumbersome Registers of Births overflowing with that name. Most hailed from Wales but the 1901 census shows our William's place of birth as Notting Hill in London.

One London entry for 21st July 1860 records a Charlotte Williams giving birth to a boy named William at Alfred Place, Westbourne Park. The father (also William) was a commercial traveller who died before the baby was registered. An entry for 1st April 1861 offers a starker reminder of the more wretched alternatives available to single mothers in Victorian England, wherein Emma Williams gave birth to another William at the Kensington Workhouse. Twenty days later and less than a mile away, another William Williams was born at The Duke of Sussex Public House in Latymer Road, where Isaac Williams had been publican for six years. This is our Billy Williams.

He was the fourth child born to Isaac Williams and his wife, Susan. Isaac came from Cornwall and Susan from Dawlish in Devon; so much for one disparaging presumption that the English had to rely on a man of Welsh antecedents to find their national rugby ground. Collectively known as Notting Dale, the area of London that Billy Williams was born into was variously described by Dickens and a host of other Victorian observers as a den of filth and depravity. So appalling were the slums festering amongst brick kilns, piggeries and tanneries that the combined pollution blighted neighbouring Notting Hill to the extent that streets of half-finished houses were left to rot. On his Poverty Map of London, the Victorian social surveyor Charles Booth classified the area as inhabited by the 'lowest class, vicious and semi-criminal element'.

The Duke of Sussex was marginally less ill-positioned on the corner of Clifton Street and Latymer Road. The immediate clientele were drawn from a mixture of 'comfort and poverty'. Such was Billy Williams's introduction to the world. Little would Isaac and Susan have dreamed that one day their fourth child would cross the social divide to become a member of the MCC, play cricket for his country and become a legend in the ambitions of the Rugby Football Union. Little wonder, too, that Billy Williams later claimed the more salubrious Notting Hill address as his place of birth.

By the age of 10, Billy was beginning his formal education at Buxton College, a modest commercial establishment drawn from the pages of Dickens. Perched beside the main railway line into London at Stratford New Town, then 'the gateway to Essex', the 50 boy boarders, drawn mostly from the London area, were governed by Mr and Mrs Randle, schoolmaster and schoolmistress respectively, assisted by four other teaching staff, three of whom were working at the college to qualify for a degree.

In 1881, Williams was 20 years old and making his way in the world. Whether or not he started out on a career in property is not known, but it was his talent for sport nurtured during his schooldays that was to be the key to his success. As a young man of 25 he was appearing as wicketkeeper for Middlesex and during the winter of 1896/7, toured the West Indies with Arthur Priestley's team, finishing second in the bowling averages to A E Stoddart. Often assisting the MCC, Williams was credited with taking 100 or more wickets in a season; a record he was to maintain in all matches for 55 years. By 1900 he was financially independent and was living the life of a carefree, bachelor playboy, giving wonderful parties at his fine house in Walpole Road, Twickenham, and playing cricket occasionally for the MCC.

Elected onto the RFU Committee in 1905, Williams was briefly chairman of the new ground committee in 1907 but then faded into obscurity, save the legacy of his celebrated 'Cabbage Patch'. Sometime after 1910 Williams moved to 219 Richmond Road in Twickenham and nine years later was living at number 85, by which time he had married Sarah and had a son, Leonard. In 1924 he was made a Vice President of the RFU and the following year, aged 64, visited the West Indies during the tour of the Hon. F S G Calthorpe's MCC team, where his physical prowess was proven in Georgetown when he challenged a West Indian friend against whom he had played 30 years before to a single-wicket match for £25 a side. Winning the toss, Williams severely punished his opponent's bowling, completed a century and declared. Then, with a googly, he bowled his exhausted victim first ball.

Retiring from the RFU in 1925, Williams saw out his last summer as a cricketer in 1934 when he turned out at the age of 74 for the MCC against the House of Lords. After dismissing Lord Dalkeith, Lord

Tennyson and Major L George for 16 runs, Williams was presented by the Marylebone Club with the ball. In 1949, to celebrate the 40th anniversary of the opening of Twickenham rugby ground, the RFU Committee agreed that a letter should be sent to Williams from the President 'thanking him for all he did as the Pioneer of a Rugby Union National Ground, and actually finding the site at Twickenham'. A year later, Admiral Sir Percy Royds, Chairman of the RFU Laws Committee, considered that a more formal mark of recognition was due the man 'mainly responsible for the acquisition of the property'. It was agreed that a photograph of Billy Williams (now on display in the Twickenham Museum) should be placed in the committee room.

This turned out to be a timely gesture as Billy Williams died soon after, on 14th April 1951, at his home in Hampton Wick. For some reason, news filtered late to the RFU, which paid a belated tribute to a long life devoted to sport and the man who 'ended a long search for a suitable site for a National Rugby Union ground'. As the man who discovered 'a cabbage field of 10 acres, which has since developed into the famous Twickenham enclosure', *The Times* described 'a fine all-round player of games, as good a judge as he was player and a delightful personality'. An honorary member of the Wimbledon Park golf club, Williams played a daily round until his death.

Until then, 'age – even unfitness – seemed to have passed him by... Many will find it hard to believe that 'Billy' Williams, as he had been known for two generations, will not be seen, as erect as ever, hale and hearty, at such homes of sport as Lord's and the Athletic Ground at Old Deer Park at Richmond'. *Wisden's Directory* accurately predicted that the name of Billy Williams would 'always be associated in Rugby history with the Home Ground… as the first to see the possibilities of the RFU site at Twickenham'.

Curiously, the passing of this local hero failed to make the pages of the local press. Williams had moved to a modest semi-detached Edwardian villa in Hampton Wick sometime before 1949, without Sarah or Leonard. His death certificate includes no spouse or next or kin, only the person present at the time. Yet, six months after his death, the RFU received an application for financial assistance from Williams's solicitors on behalf of his widow, which would seem to indicate that he had either left no provision for her or that she felt some form of remuneration was due. Unfortunately, the Union's by-laws did 'not allow for contributions being made for such proposals' and the application was denied. Nothing else is known about what happened to Sarah or Leonard.

Alf Wright was first asked if he would like to help out at Twickenham through the 1919 season. A year later he was offered a permanent job at the ground for the princely sum of £1 a week. The offer was accepted and Alf stayed with the Rugby Football Union for the next 65 years. Rising to the rank of Assistant Secretary and later the RFU's first archivist, Alf Wright became the chief protector of 'any nonsense' talked about Billy Williams and his 'Cabbage Patch'.

He described Williams as 'a thoroughly Dickensian figure'; something of an entrepreneur, 'perhaps not quite a Mr Pancks, or even a Josh Bagstock, but certainly a man of affairs'. Mr Pancks is the comical rent collector in Charles Dickens's *Little Dorrit* who assists in finding William Dorrit's fortune. Josh (or Major) Bagstock is again good fun as the military vulgarian of social pretensions in *Dombey and Son*.

Shoulder to shoulder with the cream of society, we can appreciate something of the Major Bagstock analogy. 'If you had a few more of the Bagstock breed among you,' the 'tough, hard-hearted and devilishly sly operator' says of himself, 'you'd be none the worse for it.'

As to Mr Pancks, Williams was in part a 'collector of rents' (he owned at least two houses in the Twickenham area) and just as Pancks saved William Dorrit from financial disaster, so did Billy Williams save the reputation of William Cail. The social divide between the two men was profound. Williams was the son of a Notting Dale publican and Cail the quintessential product of Victorian upper middle-class society. But such is the inherent democracy of sport that celebrity and achievement can remedy what might be otherwise lacking in background.

Chapter Two

THE CABBAGE PATCH

Everyone loves a sporting hero, and on and off the field of play Billy Williams was every inch that. He played halfback for Harlequins, was a celebrated rugby referee and played cricket for his country. He served on the prestigious MCC and RFU committees alongside men of substance and breeding; the right sort. William Cail had the influence and a reputation for getting things done. Billy Williams was a streetwise accommodator. Together, they made the perfect partnership. The vision of a home ground for England Rugby was William Cail's and Billy Williams's Cabbage Patch at Twickenham was to be (in part) his salvation.

With his intimate knowledge of sporting venues and the real estate market, Billy Williams should have been more able than most to judge exactly the practicalities and (perhaps more importantly) the pitfalls in the selection of a national sporting venue. Cail wanted a site in or around London, which Williams would scout out during the course of his normal business. As Cail worked on the business plan, so began the journey that would take the Rugby Football Union from its offices in The Strand and deep into the watery wilds of west Middlesex on the wrong side of the river.

As any estate agent will testify, the mantra of the property game is Location, Location, Location. Second only to the location is accessibility, and then there is the price of the land. Historically, football grounds were mostly attracted to low value sites close to good communication links, with the space required determined by the size of the playing area. Unlike an athletics arena, football stadia require far less peripheral space for fewer players with fewer facilities. The Greeks and the Romans conceived the amphitheatre as spectator architecture thousands of years ago, which became the chosen design of football clubs as the most appropriate showcase for their sport.

More than 80 purpose-built grounds had been built in Britain by the time Billy Williams set out on his quest in 1906. He was not therefore embarking on some new voyage of discovery. Nor were his choices in any way limited by location, despite the fact that London at the turn of the 20th century was expanding at an alarming rate. From Lord's to Blackheath, Crystal Palace to The Oval, and west of London from White City to Wimbledon, vast tracts of land remained available and suitable for Cail's ambition.

While we are left with no record of Williams's 'year-long quest', a few clues survive that allow us to trace his search for a likely contender. Talk in recent years of the RFU sharing a site with the Football Association at a new Wembley Stadium has some resonance with history. Since the 1880s, the Metropolitan Railway (the original underground line) had extended out into the north Middlesex countryside as part of a visionary scheme to provide a route for the Great Central Railway Company linking Manchester with London. In an attempt to encourage more Londoners to use its railway, the company looked to build a great attraction north of Baker Street. In this they saw the potential of the Wembley Park Leisure Grounds.

This 219-acre site already boasted football and cricket pitches and a running track as well as landscaped recreational grounds. But something else was needed to encourage more people to journey out into the countryside north of the capital. In 1889 this took the form of a competition to build an attraction in the form of a 'Great Tower' for London. With the first stage at 155 feet completed in 1896, the money ran out and the stump quickly became known as 'Watkin's Folly', after the Chairman of the Metropolitan Railway whose idea it was. The site lay dormant and became something of a long-running national joke.

At the same time Billy Williams was into his quest, Watkin's Folly was being dismantled. Building the national stadium for England Rugby would have salvaged Watkin's pride, and his original concept, and afforded the Rugby Football Union an accessible location linked to the north with ease of access for the Scots, the Welsh and the Irish. Whereas Wembley enjoyed the immediate prospect of cheap return fares on the new 'Metro Electric Service' from central London, the Twickenham ground was to wait 20 years for the first omnibus to pass by its gates and was never to be blessed with close tube or rail links. By 1906, much of London's railway infrastructure (under as well as over ground) was either already in place, expanding or fast developing, except at Twickenham.

Touch Judge, the *Daily Mirror's* rugby writer, suggested that the Stamford Bridge Athletics Ground was a lost opportunity. Opened in 1877, it was used almost exclusively for the first 23 years of its life as an arena by the London Athletic Club. In 1904 the owners acquired additional land (formerly a market garden) with the aim of establishing a football team on the 12-acre site. Initially the stadium was offered to Fulham

FC but they turned it down. Instead, a new team, Chelsea FC, moved into the new Stamford Bridge stadium. The ground capacity was originally planned to be 100,000, the second largest in the country behind the Crystal Palace Arena.

Blackheath and Richmond were considered the only grounds in or near London where the finer points of the rugby football game could be appreciated. With its superior transport links, the choice of Richmond would have met with universal approval. Cail later reported that the leases on both Blackheath and Richmond were secure. Doubtless they were, although in reality Cail enjoyed nowhere near the budget required to purchase sites of such quality. His assertion, however, that both sites 'would soon be lost to the game of rugby', thus implying both were ripe for development, was simply a red herring. In fact, with a budget in the region of £8,000, Cail's options were strictly limited.

That attention turned from the Surrey to the Middlesex side of the river was later explained in so far as Twickenham already enjoyed a reputation as essentially a rugby area and having the RFU ground there would only enhance that reputation. Thus, a parcel of land considered 'excellent for rugby' was considered in the form of the 10-acre Ivy Bridge estate purchased in 1904 by market gardener Thomas Edward Mann. Bounded by the London/Twickenham Road to the east, Whitton Road and Oak Lane (now Rugby Road) to the west, it included an access road leading to the Ivy Bridge tram stop where a proper ground entrance could be built. It had all the attributes for a football ground, especially a north/south pitch alignment, and, more importantly, it was within Cail's meagre budget.

The useful source of additional income aside, an

unspecified press cutting reproduced in H B T (Teddy) Wakelam's *Harlequin Story* celebrates one of the Rugby Union's elite 'with the game being played by them in such an entertaining way, they would be able to do splendid missionary work in keeping the game alive and adding to its popularity'.

In December 1906 Cail approached RFU president, G Rowland Hill, with his idea for a home ground for the English game. Without hesitation, Hill formally proposed that Cail's finance committee should 'consider the advisability and practicality of the Union purchasing a ground in or near London'. Cail would report back 'as soon as possible with as many facts and figures as could be obtained'.

Three months later, on 15th March 1907, Cail submitted his proposal on six handwritten pages of his personal notepaper bearing the address of his Newcastle home. He calculated that of 22 matches played between 1895 and 1905, those played in London included 12 minor matches, which had cost the Union £199 for extra stands and in grants to the ground owners. The remainder had been internationals across which the Union had spent £1,947 on increased accommodation and £825 in grants. This amounted to an annual expenditure of around £3,000, which did not include the upkeep of the Union's offices in The Strand. And then there was the Union's capital languishing in the bank. If this was converted into land in or near London, Cail maintained, it would bring about a much better return over time than interest from the bank.

The sale of the Union's investments in government funded stocks, added to the probable available balance at the end of the 1907 season, equalled a sum in the region of £7,500, or just over two years' expenditure in renting grounds in London. The evidence was overwhelming. If any doubts were raised or questions asked, then these were not recorded. The motion was carried without further discussion and William Cail was given full powers to purchase a ground with immediate effect.

By this time into his fourteenth year as honorary treasurer, Cail must have known intimately the exact state of the Union's finances. Yet he later revealed that when the Union's £6,000 investments ('some bought at £110') were sold, they produced only £4,919, a shortfall of £1,081, even though there had been no sudden downturn in the economy. Indeed, the general level of the Consol yield before 1914 remained remarkably constant and the profit rate was higher. This not only left a considerable shortfall in Cail's projected budget, but something of a hole in the subsequent history of events.

The RFU's profit on games for the 1906/7 season was around £1,905, excluding the Union's financial responsibilities to member clubs. Added to this, the balance realised from the sale of the Union's investments would have produced around £6,824 or just under £700 short of target, a significant amount then. Insufficient funds meant one of three things; abandonment of the scheme, a reduction in the asking price of the land or an alternative, cheaper site.

Cail was by nature a pragmatist and so when presented with a problem – provided the investment promised reward – he sought to solve it. On 1st June 1907, just eight weeks after his submission to the Union, the *Richmond and Twickenham Times* afforded a column inch headlined 'Proposed New Rugby Ground', reporting: 'At the annual general meeting of the Rugby Football Union, held at the Inns of Court Hotel,

London, on Thursday evening, it was announced that the Union had signed an agreement for the purchase of ten acres of ground at Twickenham, and had made a ten per cent deposit'.

A few days later and a more fulsome account appeared in the *Thames Valley Times* wherein that paper's representative failed to understand why the RFU had chosen the site it did and had refused the far superior Ivy Bridge, especially when the terms for both were reported to be 'almost identical'. Despite much probing, few answers were forthcoming. What few facts could be established had to be 'gleaned from other sources'. Negotiations had been partly carried out by the local firm of Messrs Hoskins and Booth of Twickenham, but 'upon this point' the Rugby Union Committee 'preserved a stony silence'.

A sketch plan was produced by the Union describing 'The Fairfield Estate', situated a few hundred yards from the preferred Ivy Bridge site. This area of 'about ten acres' came complete with reference to a spurious 'projected electric car route' running along Whitton Road and a proposed road leading off the same. Clearly designed to present the most optimistic portrayal of a site far removed from the ideal, it was all that William Cail could afford. Also, despite what was reported in the local press, the RFU held only 8.9 acres and not 10.5. That Cail had somehow arranged special terms and conditions leads to the motivation of the vendor who was either desperate to be rid of the land or was a good friend of the RFU, sympathetic to both its aims and its tenuous financial situation.

Alf Wright denied that the Twickenham ground was ever a cabbage patch and that Billy Williams was the owner. Given that the term 'Cabbage Patch' was only ever a derisory slur, the question mark over its original ownership becomes all the more intriguing when, 90 years after its purchase, another Billy Williams emerged. In recalling his life and times in the buffer zone between Twickenham and Hounslow that is Whitton, arguably where the Rugby Ground is actually located, he made an astonishing claim:

'George Williams was my grandfather's eldest son, my uncle. They farmed the land… they leased all that land… that was Billy Williams's only ground… he leased the ground to my grandfather… he negotiated and then eventually it was all passed over to Billy Williams – the owner – to do the completion of the business.'

As a serving committee member of the Rugby Football Union at the time, the small matter of probity would have required Billy Williams to make a formal declaration to this effect. At the very least, other committee members would have required an assurance that there was no question of profiteering on the part of Billy Williams or collusion between him and William Cail. That the RFU maintained an ominous 'stony silence' and refused to be drawn on detail, might explain the ambiguities surrounding the purchase, with specific regard to the favourable terms and conditions obtained by Cail.

According to family legend, George and Billy Williams were either brothers or brothers-in-law. Despite the veracity of our informant's overall testimony, such a dramatic piece of breaking news requires the establishment of exactly what was the relationship, if any, between the two men. After all, it would have been one thing to have kept the details surrounding the deal firmly in-house, but quite another to expect the probing representative of the *Thames Valley Times* not to have discovered such a link between the famous local sportsman and a close relative who just happened to have been farming the land purchased by the RFU for their new ground.

From around 1875, numerous branches of the clan Williams settled in the Twickenham area. As well as those from Aldershot and Birmingham, of three branches arriving from Colchester, Essex, one included George Williams, a market gardener and the grandfather of the informant. By 1891 he had moved his growing family from one cottage in Twickenham to another on the Richmond Road. There he stayed with his wife, Ellen, and their eight children until on 29th September 1903, he took out a 21-year lease on Orchard Cottage, Whitton Road. Although its mid-19th-century contemporaries survive along Whitton Road, Orchard Cottage was cleared along with its 1.9-acre orchard to be replaced by the large house on the corner of what is today Tayben Avenue.

The only evidence to suggest that George Williams did farm part of the site was the access road cut into it directly opposite Orchard Cottage, probably in 1904, the same year that Lot 7 of 12 other lots of 'Whitton Lands' were put up for auction. However, despite all of this tantalising 'evidence', Billy Williams was not the owner of the land acquired by the RFU. Neither were his great friends, the extensive Mann family who owned or leased much of the land in the area. Nor Frank Peacock, another major contender, who was described in his obituary following a freak accident in 1939 as 'the old market gardener that cultivated the Rugby Union Ground'. The owner was in fact the Right Honourable Charles Seale-Hayne, MP, who died in 1904.

Lot 7 was one of three plots that failed to make their reserve, itself an ominous sign. It was eventually sold off to a consortium, which provided Cail his opportunity. The deed held at the offices of the RFU's lawyers states that on 9th August 1907, John Frazer Donald, Esq., of East Lodge, Melrose Road, Wandsworth, Surrey, of the First Part; Jonathan Donald of Primrose Hill, Witham, Essex, of the Second Part; and Mary Donald of East Lodge, Melrose Road, Wandsworth, Surrey, of the Third Part, conveyed to William Cail, Esq., of Cail's Buildings, Newcastle, Northumberland; Charles Arnold Crane of Manor House, Borlingham, Pershore, Worcs; Edward Temple Guidon of 28 Lincoln's Inn Fields, London, Solicitor; John Hammond, 9 Old Square, Lincoln's Inn, London, Barrister; and Arthur Hartley of County Chambers, Castleford, York (purchaser of the Fourth Part), pieces of land situated in Twickenham in the County of Middlesex.

The bulk of the estate to the south belonged to John Frazer Donald, with the remaining third in red to the north to Mary Donald, and part owned by Joseph Cape, valued at £2,000 with £2,050 remaining owing to John Frazer Donald and Joseph Cape on the security of the indenture up to the death of those two. The total purchase price as of 1st July 1904 was £5,572 12s. 6d, which included £4,072 12s. 6d. for the northern third of the land plus £1,500.

With Land Registry dated 31st August 1907, 1st March 1909 and 1st July 1924, thus was the wily RFU Treasurer able to secure a foothold and bring about his commitment to secure a ground for England Rugby. However, as much as Billy Williams broke every rule in the sports ground realty book as far as his choice of location was concerned, so Cail's expediency over vigilance meant that the Rugby Football Union was to pay dearly for decades to come with regard to poor access and expansion of the ground.

As far as can be established, Billy and George Williams were not related by blood or marriage. Acting as he was on behalf of the RFU, the 'completion of the business' would have rightly been given over to Billy Williams in his professional capacity. Both men, however, would have doubtless known each other, and perhaps given Billy's celebrity and the shared surname, more was made of their relationship as the story of the rugby ground was passed down.

Immediately it was considered 'mad' to site the Rugby Football Union's national stadium '13 miles from Piccadilly Circus – in the middle of nowhere'. Twickenham railway station, which at best offered only a mediocre service, was a good mile away. No omnibus or tram routes ran to, from or via the site. 'No history attached the place,' declared one newspaper. 'It was once a cabbage patch,' bemoaned another, 'utterly unsuited for Rugby football because of the heavy, water-retaining properties of land on the Twickenham side of the river.'

Given the punctilious nature of the RFU and its attention to detail with regard to the game itself, the timescale afforded this scheme from proposal through to purchase was, at the very least, uncharacteristically hasty and throughout displayed almost breathtaking indifference. But like many a successful manager, William Cail knew the value of delegation. Crucially he was a survivor. Billy Williams was a man who enjoyed the bouquets and had the skin to endure the brickbats.

In fairness to both men, many a club had taken on sites far from ideal. St Andrews, Ninian Park, Maine Road, Burnden Park and The Valley were all originally rubbish dumps, disused quarries or pits. Craven Cottage and White Hart Lane were overgrown wildernesses. And Hillsborough, like Twickenham, was sited in an outlying region far from the city centre. But at Twickenham it was the sheer tangle of adverse environmental, geographical and geological problems that opened the door to continued criticism. As a local land agent, Billy Williams would have known that the entire area north of Twickenham station was under constant threat of flooding.

The Duke of Northumberland's river marking the western boundary of the ground was cut after the Reformation as an artificial tributary from the River Crane to service the mills at Isleworth. On Tuesday 16th June 1903, after heavy rainfalls and the rapid rise of the water in the Crane, both rivers broke their banks and flooded vast areas of low-lying ground in the surrounding district. The Duke's River overflowed down Oak Lane (now Rugby Road) towards St Margaret's. Carts were stationed both sides of Chase Bridge to convey people along the Whitton Road. By 6 pm on Wednesday the water had receded. Such was the choice of location for the RFU's new ground.

Then there was the site's close proximity to the Heston & Isleworth sewage works. Now the Mogden Water Purification complex, covering an area the size of a small town, its embryonic odour at the turn of the last century was no less onerous, as one local correspondent put it to the *Richmond and Twickenham Times* in 1902.

And then there was the business of actually getting to and from the ground. Before the 1930s there was no Chertsey arterial road and no Twickenham Bridge. Having reached the area by whatever means, getting to the rugby ground meant traversing narrow, winding country lanes where no buses or trams ran. One local estate agent positively celebrated this profound lack of transport infrastructure, proclaiming: 'no noisy tramcar or motor omnibus to make both the day and night hideous, and the lives of your wives and children unsafe, but absolute country quiet and seclusion within 29 minutes of London's centre'.

Supporters of the new ground looked to Kneller Hall where, according to the founder member of Richmond Rugby Club, Edwin Ash, 'military bandsmen and bandmasters had for half a century been posted without a feeling of remoteness, then surely rugby men could do the same.' Ash was one of O L Owen's 'elder RFU statesmen' who shared the vision and gave Cail's scheme 'the necessary backing'. When Ash first came to the area in 1861, he worked at a military academy. This might have been the officers' preparation school for Sandhurst facing Richmond Green, or the Royal Military School of Music at Kneller Hall in Whitton, which he famously noted as 'already established within a stone's throw of the site and the halt at Twickenham'.

In his history of the Rugby Football Union, Owen claims that 'in 1907, Rugby Football at Twickenham was an experiment and that at the time it was impossible to do more than to erect two covered stands and limited terracing'. An experiment is a scientific test done to prove or disprove something; an analysis of new information gathered by observation or experimentation. Yet, conceived as it was towards the end of the boom years in British football stadium building, Twickenham was no experiment.

Had Cail secured the Richmond Athletic Ground then he would today bask in the glory. That he purchased its antithesis saw Billy Williams, the loyal Union man, shoulder the responsibility. Alf Wright maintained it was Billy Williams who 'suggested that the

Union might like to buy the site, despite the protestations of those who thought he was mad'. While 'this did not stop Billy', the ultimate decision was never his. The notion of experiment was 'spun' as a face-saving expedient; a fallback position should the deficiencies of the site have resulted in complete disaster for Cail and his scheme. The responsibility for what has grown into a high status stadium was William Cail's and his alone. Had he shouldered that responsibility from the outset then possibly it would be his name associated with the glory that has grown from Billy Williams's Cabbage Patch.

Chapter Three

LAYING THE FOUNDATIONS

Not all of the RFU hierarchy was convinced that their money was well spent. No reason was given for the sudden resignation of Percy Coles, a former Oxford Blue, who was appointed the first paid Secretary of the RFU in 1904 with offices found for him at 35 Surrey Street, just off The Strand. A hint as to his departure following the acquisition of the ground is contained in Owen's account of Cail's requirements for 'like-minded, able-bodied individuals to help ensure the venture's ultimate success'. Specifically, Cail wanted the fearsome Charles Marriott, 'a forceful personality on and off the field' and a legendary figure of the England game. Owen credits William Cail as seeing Marriott through his new role as Secretary; a mentoring process that doubtless started well before his appointment.

By September 1907, the work of clearing and fencing the site was begun and the 'fine collection of fruit trees' torn down in readiness for the task of laying the first Twickenham pitch. A month later, newly elected President of the Rugby Football Union, Charles Crane, made his first visit to the site accompanied by the Ground Committee and William Cail. The main business of the day was to go over the ground to 'inspect chairs and levels etc', to ascertain the layout and elevation vital for the appreciation of the finer points of the game, where venues such as the vast Crystal Palace Arena failed miserably.

Long used by the RFU for internationals, Joseph Paxton's glass and iron masterpiece was set on a rise that overlooked the park. The football pitch was laid out in 1895 on the bed of a former artificial lake. Here the vast majority of spectators were crammed onto the sloping grassy banks without any terracing or crush barriers, many fifty or more yards from the touchline. Viewing was less than adequate if the crowd was large, which made it 'not at all suitable for watching the intricacies of the game of rugby'. When it was wet the slopes turned into slippery banks of mud, and the pitch had considerable drainage problems.

Charles Crane's reaction to the Union's fledgling site is not recorded. The meeting then adjourned in the direction of Twickenham Junction and the Railway Hotel (now The Cabbage Patch) to meet with Architect, J C A Greatorex, to discuss 'the completion of the stands'. Although fees were being paid, no formal plans were as yet drawn up. The Ground Committee took with them a payment of £3,500, which was minuted as completing the purchase, but which Cail, in his later autobiographical notes, explained was in fact only a first payment. Clearing, fencing, legal charges and architect's fees already amounted to £1,250, which, when added to this £3,500 payment left little change from Cail's paltry budget.

The date set aside for the first match (8th February 1908) was hugely optimistic even by Cail's standards. Whereas the clearing and peripheral work was presenting few difficulties, the business of laying out the pitch was to bring home the true magnitude of the undertaking. The axis of a football ground is an important factor in terms of natural ventilation in allowing for the drying of the pitch by the wind and sun. Here the site was excellent in providing the best orientation of the 'ends' alignment. And while the overall design of a stadium is important, so too is what lies underground, in the substructure and drainage. Despite the initial effort required to fill and level disused rubbish dumps or quarry pits, a sub-layer of ash and clinker creates an economical and effective form of drainage. Otherwise, an expensive drainage system is required.

Indeed, no sooner had the first spade become bonded to the glutinous blue-clay subsoil than William Cail found himself faced with yet another stark choice. Either extra funding had to be found or the grand gesture faltered at the first failed shovel-full. To this end, if Cail's handwritten proposal for an England ground represents the most important document in the Twickenham Archive, then his joint letter with Charles Crane in February 1908 is the second. Ostensibly a progress report to member counties and clubs on the 'formation of a first-class football ground', superfluous detail is skilfully avoided, except to think it 'of interest to state' that in spite of recent heavy rainfall the ground was in excellent condition with 'no signs of water accumulation or flooding'. Clearly, word had spread about the dubious nature of the site. As ever and looking beyond such mundane considerations, Cail focused on his vision of a 'better class' of ground.

What he proposed was two covered stands, each 330 feet long and seating about 4,000 spectators, with double that number standing. In all there would be accommodation for roughly 20,000 spectators. One stand would be complete with players' dressing and bathrooms, offices, committee and luncheon rooms, and a kitchen. Press seats would be included and a telegraph office. The overall site would be complete with proper entrance gates and turnstiles, and all utilities. A prize was to be advertised for the most suitable design. However, for the Union to accomplish all of this, a further £10,000 was required to be realised by First Mortgage Debentures of £50, each bearing interest of five per cent. Cail hoped that member counties and clubs would raise £8,000, which would be added to the acquisition and start-up costs as well as several other undisclosed 'costly improvements'.

In the event, only £5,700 was raised, of which £2,400 came from committee members, £1,600 from a few county unions and clubs, £1,550 from old players and £150 from outsiders. Two committee members previously resolved to taking out debentures changed their minds, thereby undermining Cail's basis for borrowing from the bank. After openly 'outing' his errant colleagues, one of them rescinded and recommitted to the scheme.

A report by Wharton Consulting in 2001 suggested that Cail was 'embarrassed' by this episode and even that he found himself in 'dishonest circumstances'. More likely others shared the same misgivings about the venture as did RFU Secretary Coles, who resigned. Undaunted, Cail then secured a £6,000 bank loan. This meant that by March 1908 – exactly one year after he had proposed the scheme – well over double the projected budget had dribbled into the RFU's funds, and was pouring out at a rate of knots. Thus far, the ground was fenced off with gates erected and access roads built. Some legal and architect's fees had been paid and a single payment had been made on the ground. That same month plans for the 'New Football Stands at Twickenham' were submitted to Twickenham

Urban District Council by the firm of architects and surveyors, J E Profit, Henderson and Brown; Mr Greatorex having shifted his responsibilities to the drawing up of 'an elaborate drainage system'. Both plans were approved on 23rd July 1908 and shortly afterwards work began in earnest.

A pitch described as dead level was made up of turf of 'the best possible description' taken from nearby Whitton Park, capable of 'standing any amount of wear and tear'. Belying its true nature, the soil beneath it was described as a rich loam, which complemented an – as yet untested – 'perfect' drainage system. As much greeted an enthusiastic representative of *Athletic News* towards the end of 1908 who announced 'a field of play ready for action'. The stand foundations were finished and the Union was awaiting 'the official hallmark' to proceed with their plans. Hopes abounded that the ground would be ready for the more important matches of the coming 1908/9 season, 'but, as a consequence of the action of the local authorities, who appear to have been trained in the Circumlocution Office,' sighed the paper's representative, 'like the Scotsman "I ha' ma doots"'.

Charles Marriott was a man clearly frustrated by the delays. In a robust rebuttal of doubts surrounding adequate transport links, Marriott maintained that the new ground was far more accessible than Blackheath, 'which, until the Richmond enclosure was laid out, was the Home of Rugby in the south of England'. The new ground enjoyed the original access way off Whitton Road, which now served as the main entrance. Also two other sets of gates had been installed along Oak Lane (now Rugby Road), forming the embryonic North and East entrances for supporters coming from the direction of Brentford and Isleworth. Here was a

Rugby Football Union eager to see their enterprise up and running, reported *Athletic News*.

The motor omnibus was almost universal after 1905, but horse-drawn and steam omnibuses continued on the roads until well after the First World War. Plenty of such public transport flowed to and from Twickenham over Richmond Bridge, which was often jammed on bank holidays with special services to Hurst Park for a day at the races. But no buses ran towards Whitton and the 'New Football Ground' and while Twickenham railway station was a mere five minutes further from Waterloo than Richmond, there was a good ten-minute crawl from there to the ground.

Overhead electric traction first ran to outer London in July 1901 and trams came to Twickenham in 1903. With regard to Charles Marriott's 'splendid service of trams' serving the new ground, there was a stop at Ivy Bridge on the Twickenham and London Road from the direction of Hammersmith, but before the days of the A316 Chertsey arterial and other roads cutting through the mass of market gardens, this meant a convoluted eight-to-ten-minute walk to the ground via Twickenham Junction or Mogden Lane.

Marriott had been confident of the England trial matches and the Australian fixtures being played at the new ground on 9th January, but now could not even hazard a guess as to when a start could be made. 'If we had a free hand,' he grumbled, 'we should be ready in about eight weeks.' Since the stands were not yet built, the Union was clearly proposing to arrange matches using the foundations and mounds as temporary terracing, which in itself carried statutory health and safety implications. Whereas the actual stability of a ground was not within the local authority remit, it was contained in the Public Health Act of 1890. The Council therefore had no option but to decline to 'express their satisfaction' as to use of the ground for 9th January 1909.

Although local regulations abounded at this time, planning permission did not exist. A borough surveyor could only report on building work proceeding at the risk of the owner and items that infringed the council's by-laws. Following questions by council members, the borough surveyor was asked to clarify the reasons for the delay and exactly what tests were required. In this, reference to the lack of provision of 'all appliances' presumably referred to the toilet arrangements. An Act of 1907 already enforced their provision in new grounds, but not to improvements where they already existed.

Deeply unimpressed by all of this, the man from *Athletic News* preferred to report Marriott's version of events rather than the facts of the matter, which was that the Secretary and new Ground Manager was himself partly responsible for the delays. Marriott believed that it was safer not to take risks, which was commendable and very responsible, but no mention was made of this, or William Cail's protracted correspondence with the firm of architects, reminding them of their contractual responsibilities, despite the Fates conspiring to sink the ship carrying the steel girders for the stands from Glasgow.

The *Athletic News* representative also chose to lambast the 'foolish actions' of local people unable to appreciate the money-making potential of the new ground. Although no voices of dissent were to be found either in the local press or council proceedings, doubtless some of the wealthier and more influential members of local society in the comfortable villas sandwiched between the ground and Whitton Road were less than delighted at the prospect of a football stadium literally in their own back yards.

Meanwhile, the Scottish Rugby Union had decided not to play England for the Calcutta Cup on the grounds that the game south of the border was tainted with professionalism. Some English clubs, so the Scots alleged, had paid their players over and above legitimate expenses, which the RFU vehemently denied. If in retaliation the RFU decided not to allow affiliated clubs to play any Scottish teams then it would have proved disastrous for county games, especially London Scottish who played at Richmond. Added to this would have been the probability of Ireland following Scotland's lead, and Wales being placed in the same position as England. The Varsity teams would also have been affected and it was difficult to determine what the ultimate outcome would be. According to the *Richmond and Twickenham Times*, however, this was equally serious a matter for the 'new ground at Whitton', where the annual contest with Scotland was planned as the opening match. Fortunately for the future of the game the rift between the two Unions was quickly healed and the annual context went ahead at Richmond while the RFU's new ground awaited completion.

With a fresh batch of girders having eventually made their way from Glasgow, the *Morning Post* declared optimistically that 'all was now plain sailing' at the new ground. The comprehensive steelwork was hauled along the winding country lanes from Isleworth or Brentford docks by steam lorries or horse-drawn wagons and once on site manual labour positioned the girders ready for the building and infrastructure work to begin; a timely project within the context of the massive bout of unemployment blighting the nation. However, throughout the ground's construction, with council minute books bulging with requests from government and neighbouring authorities to create or find work, the only mention made of the enterprise is found on 27th May 1909, with the borough surveyor reporting that the building was going ahead in accordance with the local by-laws and with 'no infringements or offences committed'.

Not once are the work opportunities afforded by the construction referred to. In the days before mechanical diggers, and given the scale of the project, a small army of men used to wielding picks and shovels would have been required to shift the thousands of tons of soil to create the foundations, with the spoil then heaped to form the embryonic South Terrace. As many tons of concrete would have required to have been mixed before being poured into the trenches and cast into shuttered moulds to create the terraces to contain the steelwork.

Remarkably, this not insignificant workforce appeared out of nowhere and encamped or was accommodated somewhere, but no mention of it can be found in local government records or the press. The *Thames Valley Times* did look with optimism to the new ground to provide a welcome boost to the Twickenham economy it badly required. Despite its incredulity over the choice of site, the paper welcomed the news that Twickenham had been selected as the centre of England's international rugby games. With stand accommodation for 'between sixty and seventy thousand people' coming into the town several times during the winter season, it was bound to 'stimulate the whole life of the place', it declared.

Aside from the internationals there would doubtless

be other, lesser games drawing good gates, as well as other uses for the ground during the summer months in the form of other sport and athletic events. Also, Harlequins Football Club had submitted their formal application to use the new stadium as their home ground, with legendary tactician of the game, Adrian Stoop, securing an option of three years at the end of the first two. But still, and for whatever reasons, there remained a measure of antipathy between the RFU and the local authority with its unerring indifference to the scheme.

Mostly, the arrival of a football ground was as much bound up in civic pride as the public library or the town hall. All else aside, such a venture was normally viewed as a stimulant for employment in construction and maintenance, the supply of building materials and the use of local firms and labour. The *Chatham and Rochester News* wrote of New Brompton's ambitions to keep abreast of its neighbours with the building of a Technical Institute and a new safe dock, but to crown it all a football ground in the form of the Priestfield Stadium had been purchased and laid out. Roker Park enjoyed a spectacular opening with pipe bands marching through the town, steamboats on the river and Lord Londonderry officially opening the ground with a golden key.

But in the same month that Twickenham's new rugby ground was due to open, the *Richmond and Twickenham Times* carried a fulsome feature article, complete with photograph, celebrating the opening of the district's 'First Local Roller Skating Rink'. A few weeks later, a bold public announcement declared the opening ceremony of the Richmond Bridge Ice Skating Rink. But marking the opening of the district's new football ground was a meagre notice at the bottom of the *Richmond Herald* sports page, headed 'The New Rugby Ground', quoting the *Daily Mirror's* Touch Judge:

'Unless arrangements are come to with the railway authorities the ground cannot be considered as cheap and easy of access from London, and the walk from the platform into the stands, unless one desires to beat some walking records, takes roughly fifteen minutes. I do not like to throw cold water on the affair, but cannot help thinking that the Rugby union have purchased a costly white elephant. Having missed Stamford Bridge, they should have gone to Richmond.'

The Rugby Football Union's new rugby ground at Twickenham had arrived not so much quietly onto the local and national sporting scene, but more by way of an apology.

Chapter Four

OPEN FOR BUSINESS

Saturday 2nd October 1909 should have marked England Rugby's new ground's big day. Tenants Harlequins would face Richmond on the brand new field of play captained by 'that most rhythmical of passers', Adrian Stoop. Harlequins were regarded as the strongest side in London that season. As the Union's *corps d'élite*, Harlequins were expected to mark the opening of their new home ground by repeating their comprehensive win over Richmond (39-12) the previous season.

By rights it should have been a great occasion and one for celebration, but it was not. Instead, tortured tales of travelling to the ground from 'The City' dominated what sparse press reports there were. Opportunities had been lost by feckless local administration and a Rugby Football Union itself all too often silent and self-absorbed. Although the railway had come to Twickenham in 1848, so poor a service was it that by 1907 local residents had endured enough and forced the council to meet with the London & South Western Railway Company to urge improvements. It would have been in the RFU's best interests to do the same but they chose not to become involved. The Union's new ground was, after all, still only an 'experiment', which might explain their low-key approach.

The *Thames Valley Times* empathised with many a punter having to travel to Twickenham on 'a very long and, in the absence of concessions from the Railway Company, expensive journey from the City'. But then not everyone came from that direction. For while the route from Twickenham station to the ground continues to bear the most visible brunt of foot traffic, thousands more follow the myriad paths trod by pioneer spectators marked by favoured watering holes.

From the direction of Brentford and Isleworth there is The London Apprentice and, until recently, The Jolly Gardener, subsequently renamed The Triple Crown, which is now an Indian restaurant. From Hounslow town, The Bell, The Windmill and The Shire Horse are busy on match days. From Hounslow railway station, The North Star leads the way to The South Western and to Whitton's White Hart. The Duke of Cambridge opposite Kneller Hall is but a decent punt from the ground. The route march from Richmond includes The Sun, The Orange Tree, The White Cross, The White Swan and others. For those supporters coming from the direction of Isleworth Station there is the County Arms, or the Royal Oak if taking the old Oak Lane route through the delights of Mogden Water Purification Works.

H Vincent Jones, of *The Observer*, visited the ground a week before the opening to draw a 'pen picture'. He wrote that the walk to the ground 'is said to be a bare half-mile from Twickenham railway station. Perhaps that is so – as the crow flies; but to those of us who have not developed any Bleriot or Latham like tendency…this particular half-mile is longer than any of the other half-miles in that part of the world.'

The *Richmond and Twickenham Times* took a different

view. It imagined that the walk would mean little to rugby enthusiasts, although possibly 'a little uncomfortable on wet days'. The *Thames Valley Times* considered that those who objected to the 12-minute walk from Twickenham station to the New Ground would stand 'a poor chance in the Marathon'. One enterprising soul provided a large horse-drawn brake in readiness to ferry passengers between Twickenham station and the ground, but even 'at the small charge of 3d.', not a single penny was turned, which indicates that very few of those pioneer spectators shared the journalists' unremitting concerns. Almost a century later and the old station has been replaced by a concrete and glass box on the opposite side of London Road, but the walk to the ground is little changed.

Having completed 'the marathon' from Twickenham station and oozed through the bottleneck at the north end of Whitton Road, the embryonic 'Twickenham Experience' would have begun with a peek of the west roof just visible behind the row of solid Victorian villas and mature trees flanking the south end of the ground. At the junction of Whitton Road and Oak Lane (now Rugby Road), a large house occupied what the RFU describes as its 'front lawn', the grassed area that seems to have been vacant forever. Moving on up Oak Lane there was an east entrance before an acre of apple trees on land yet to be requisitioned by the Union. North of that was the groundsman's cottage and another entrance.

The main entrance was the original access road halfway along Whitton Road towards Chase Bridge. Once inside, the raised pitch was flanked west and east by a pair of covered stands dubbed A and B, each capable of seating about 3,000, with accommodation for some 24,000 standing. Seats cost four shillings, which was a lot of money at the time. As Alf Wright recalled, 'only moneyed people went to watch rugby from the grandstands in those days'.

For the less well off there was terracing at the southern end to hold about 7,000. The *Thames Valley Times* described the stand accommodation as 'extensive and very complete'. Despite its 'vast proportions', it was possible to obtain a good view of the play from any part of the ground, and contrary to criticisms, there was also sufficient flexibility to meet the demands of an international match by creating additional terracing at the north end without interfering with the sloping embankments.

The Times praised the new stands as 'excellent structures' and the enclosure as one that should become popular. H Vincent Jones for *The Observer* liked a lot of what he saw, except for the stands. They were, he decided, set too far back from the field. Nor was he impressed with the arrangements made for the comfort and convenience of the Fourth Estate; a complaint shared by colleagues from the *News of the World* and Major Philip Trevor of *The Daily Telegraph*.

They took it badly that the RFU so thoughtlessly treated 'the best friends they have – the sporting press', by having their press box facing the sun and being too far from the changing rooms, which made identifying players difficult. For not all clubs at that time 'pandered to vulgar curiosity by numbering the players'. *The Sportsman* however fell over itself in praise of the new enclosure 'replete with all modern conveniences'. As long as a Harlequins side was playing there, it declared, 'and was playing the most invigorating rugby in England, there was little danger of the public being put off by the coldness of the place'. With the pitch raised and with a proper system of drainage introduced, the *Richmond Herald* reported – a tad over-optimistically, perhaps – 'many of the objections would disappear'. But then there was the matter of the grass. Likened to 'the hair of some of our clever friends', the Twickenham pitch 'was at the opening performance, a little too artistic in the matter of length'.

It would be quite a long time, *The Times* considered, before the turf would equal that at the Richmond Athletic Ground. It accepted that the grass had to be kept very long compared with other grounds in order to protect the young turf, which had to last a long season. Although *The Observer* described the pitch as excellent, it felt it could be improved by allowing fifty sheep to wander over it. Sheep, in the paper's opinion, would knit the turf better than a roller and besides, 'a local farmer would only be too glad to allow his flock to graze there'.

The *Thames Valley Times* felt the grass was too long for fast football and trusted that 'the courteous Secretary and manager of the ground, Mr Marriott', would put it right before the next match. Sadly this trust was sorely misplaced. The *Morning Post* was less forgiving. After 'such an apology for summer', it maintained, more consideration should have been afforded the cutting of the grass and it bemoaned the lack of a scythe or mower to trim 'the splendid old turf from Whitton Park'.

The *Richmond and Twickenham Times* agreed that it would have been better had the grass been mown, but felt that 'fellow scribes' had made too much of the matter and turned to 'undoubtedly the most important Rugby match in the district...on the opening of the splendidly appointed new rugby ground at Twickenham'.

From the same unaccredited press report quoted in Wakelam's *Harlequin Story*, we learn that 'it is very probable that the only really big crowds we shall see at the Rugby Union ground will be on the occasion of the internationals, and that upon ordinary days there will appear to be little reason for this pretentious and costly arena'. Sadly, the big crowd expected, and the 'many notabilities of the Rugby Union', failed to appear. Only a few thousand spectators attended and there was no formal opening ceremony.

The game was started with G V Carey of Harlequins becoming the first man to kick off at Twickenham. Harlequins set the pace in the first twenty minutes, in which their forwards got the ball with some frequency and the backs did the scoring. Richmond's forwards would have carried the game with a little better support behind, although it was a close call, in a match between the Richmond forwards and the Harlequins' backs, with the latter having the whiphand for scoring. In the second half the Harlequins' forwards were badly beaten, but the backs were sufficiently clever to snatch another opening for a fourth try, which was converted, and sufficiently sound in defence to prevent more than two scores against them. If the Richmond pack had betrayed the same desperate energy and earnestness in the first half as in the second, it is possible that the result might have been reversed.

An exciting finish to a very good match, which saw Harlequins win by 14-10, led the *Richmond Herald* to glumly report an opening game where 'two teams just met and played'. Whereas the hypercritical will always find fault, Twickenham was voted 'an excellent home for the rugby code in England. Nothing could rob the event of its symbolism. For here, for the first time – and high time too – English Rugby had a home it can call its own.' With all the near-excitement of the first game over, bare reference was made in the press to England Rugby's national showcase. Even on the local scene reaction to Twickenham's newest and most prestigious attraction was subdued. It is difficult now to understand such a comprehensive wave of indifference accompanying the arrival of a new national stadium. But whereas a club match clearly hadn't the pulling power, the first international would confirm the ground's true potential.

Saturday 15th January 1910 was a damp, raw winter's day when England took to the field looking to beat Wales for the first time in twelve long years. Gloucester Captain D R Gent, a veteran of the 1905 England v All Blacks game, was a member of the first England team to play at Twickenham. Fifty years later as rugby correspondent for *The Times*, he recalled the 'energy, imagination, enthusiasm and courage' of all those connected with the creation of the new ground on the occasion of its first international. The teams ran on to the pitch a quarter of an hour late, keeping waiting a crowd of between twenty and thirty thousand frenzied spectators, including His Royal Highness, King George V, probably the greatest rugby fan of all the five monarchs who have reigned since Twickenham was built. The home team won the toss and 'in a couple of minutes after the kick off, this historic match was won by England!'

The opening gambit in those days was for the side that kicked off to kick up and across the field and for their forwards to follow up and prevent a clean return to touch, where the game really started. But Adrian Stoop had other ideas, and the Welshmen played right into his hands. Having taken his position about midway between the goal-line and the halfway line, the ball came straight to him. He fielded it cleanly, but then, instead of kicking, he started at once to run at top speed up the field and diagonally towards the left. Though surprised, others quickly realised what he was doing and moved up on his inside. England started passing, this time along the line towards F E Chapman on the right wing, who in a flash was over in the north-eastern corner to score, as D R Gent enthused, 'as good a try as one would ever wish to see'.

The Welsh were caught napping, leaving the door open for Chapman to become the first player to score a try in an international at Twickenham; then another first as he converted. In less than five minutes, England were seven points up and their supporters were yelling with delight, which they kept up for the rest of the match. The home team kept up the pressure, before yet another first for Chapman as he kicked a penalty goal. At once, Wales responded, this time with a try from forward, T Evans, but Jack Bancroft failed with the kick.

England fought back to end the first half 11-3, but found the second half hard going with Wales getting well under way and taking a lot of stopping. They scored once, but the kick was missed, and England hung on to beat Wales for the first time since 1898 and win the opening match at Twickenham by a goal, a penalty and a try to two tries. This, reported Gent 50 years after the event, was 'indeed the right way to open a new ground' and 'to bring English Rugby Football and its new home straight away into the limelight'.

The Observer reporter, however, was more taken with the 'uncanny acoustics', which sent 'unguarded comments' echoing around the ground. 'When the blood is up the speech is not meant for the company; much unintended phrase is spoken when an opponent has missed the ball and caught the shin.' No change there then.

Chapter Five

GRAND GESTURE OR FINAL WHISTLE?

In terms of profit, receipts from the first international netted more than £2,000. Ireland drew with England at Twickenham that same season, attracting a crowd of fewer than 14,000, but still managing to accumulate £1,700 through the turnstiles. A total of three victories and one draw went on to bring England their first championship since 1891-2. William Cail's 'great experiment at Twickenham' augured well for the future of English Rugby. In all there was little that the England rugby game could do wrong in its new home.

But two years after the RFU's original purchase, the extent of the holding at Twickenham was still only 8.9 acres. It was not until 1911 that the Union's liabilities were being paid off, and not until 1913, the same year that the Union purchased the remaining 1.6 acres, that they finally were. Harlequins, as tenants, had no reason to complain. Between 1910 and 1911, the club showed a profit of £423. This dropped to £299 in the following year, owing partly to an increased Twickenham rent. But the club's credit balance at the start of the 1912-13 season was a healthy £1,163, which represented a remarkable rise from their position some five years earlier. England meanwhile had won the Championship, shared it with Ireland in 1912, went on to twice win the Triple Crown and in 1914 won the Grand Slam.

Twickenham had brought England success; and out of this had begun a new tradition on Billy Williams's unpromising cabbage patch, ushering in a golden era of English rugby. But then, deep into the summer of 1914, when the Union was considering the business of building a North Stand, extra terracing and a clock tower, attention was rudely turned elsewhere following the assassination of an Archduke in some far off place called Sarajevo.

A matter of days after the declaration of war with Germany, all national, county and club fixtures were cancelled. As the serving President of the RFU at the time, Arthur Hartley circulated an instruction advising rugby players to volunteer to fight for their country. Of the England team that left the field of play having secured for their country its first taste of a Grand Slam, five players would not return from the unimaginable horrors of the Front. A few special games were arranged up until November 1915; otherwise the game was completely in abeyance and Twickenham lay dormant.

Throughout the global conflict, William Cail defended the home front against 'unfair' rate demands from the local authority, while Charles Marriott went off to become the oldest subaltern in France. Amongst others, Ronald W Poulton-Palmer, one of the most famous players of the day who had captained the most successful England team in decades, was killed by a sniper's bullet in 1915. Marriott survived the conflict and returned to take up where he had left off as the irascible RFU Secretary, Ground Manager and chief *aide-de-camp* to William Cail. Of sixteen matches played between 1st March and 16th April 1919, six were played at Twickenham. King George V presented the winner's Royal Trophy to New Zealand, who beat the mother country (11-3) in a replay at the ground. He watched both of the internationals at Twickenham during the 1919-1920 season when England beat France (8-3) and Scotland (13-4).

December 1921 saw the first University Match to be played at Twickenham, a move that was lamented by some who feared the loss of the intimate atmosphere of its old Queen's Club fixture. But that venue could no longer compete with the superior accommodation of numbers offered by Twickenham. Thereafter, playing the match on a Tuesday in December became a tradition. Towards the end of the 1923-4 season, England was enjoying one of its greatest seasons in a period when the rugby game was attracting more attention, with the numbers passing through the Twickenham turnstiles steadily mounting. But, as the popularity of the game increased, so too did Twickenham's shortcomings. The lack of flexibility with regard to expansion and difficult access was fast leading to Cail's grand gesture becoming a victim of its own success.

The decision was taken to utilise Leicester's Welford Road Ground where four England internationals had been played in the past. Officially this was to assess the feasibility of a return to the playing of occasional matches in the provinces. But the real reason was that a decision had to be made about accommodating ever-increasing numbers at Twickenham. Fortunately, the poor turnout at Welford Road influenced the decision to continue with Cail's great 'experiment' and to expand accommodation at Rugby HQ. The idea of building double-decker stands at the north and south ends of the ground was proposed by the engineering firm of Messrs Humphreys Ltd, of Knightsbridge, who had wide experience in the construction of sporting

William Cail, chief architect of Twickenham. (RFU)

William (Billy) Williams who found the Twickenham site. (RFU)

From humble beginnings. The Duke of Sussex (above) – Billy Williams's birthplace and (below) as a member of the RFU committee (third from right middle row). (RFU)

The waterlogged location. Whitton Road from Chase Bridge. (author)

The Railway Tavern (now the Cabbage Patch), where the New Ground Committee met. (RFU)

The irascible Secretary Charles Marriott (left) inspecting the new ground with Fred Stokes, England Rugby's first captain. (RFU)

The legendary Adrian Stoop whose wandering Harlequins found a home at Twickenham. (RFU)

George A Street (pictured above with his family) who laid out the first pitch at Twickenham and Charles Hale (below) the groundsman for many years. (RFU)

A view of the new ground towards the 'A' (West) Stand. (RFU)

THE FIRST MATCH AT TWICKENHAM (Harlequins 14pts. Richmond 10pts.), 2 October 1909. *Standing:* G. R Maxwell-Dove, J. H. Denison, B. H. Bonham-Carter, G. V. Carey, W. G. Beauchamp, T. Potter, R. E. Hancock, R. O C. Ward. *Seated:* H. J. H. Sibree, D. Lambert, A. D. Stoop (capt.), W. A. Smith (pres.), J. G. G. Birkett, J. G. Bussell R. W. Poulton. *In front:* F. M. Stoop, G. M. Chapman.

Saturday 2nd October 1909. Harlequins ready to meet Richmond for the first-ever game at Twickenham. (RFU)

G V Carey for Harlequins is the first man to kick off at Twickenham.
Quins beat Richmond 14-10.(British Library)

Saturday 15th January 1910. Cheering England fans at the first international. (British Library)

1910. England beat Wales (11-6) for the first time in 12 years. (British Library)

Omnibuses ran from London to Twickenham Town, but nowhere near the new ground.

Twickenham in the '20s. Above, a new stand gleaming white is added to the north end. Below, it's designer, the doyen of sports stadia architecture, Archibald Leitch. (Malavan Media)

The South Terrace where the spirit of Twickenham was said to dwell and the first-ever live BBC sports radio commentary took place (15th January 1927). (RFU)

An early BBC Outside Broadcast truck at Twickenham. (RFU)

The success of the ground led to the perennial problems of parking and expansion. (RFU)

By 1931 vast iron-clad double-decker stands dominate the Twickenham skyline. (RFU)

stadia. Their contracts included stands and terracing for Reading Football Club, the Irish Rugby Union at Dublin and Exeter City.

However, while it was eminently possible to provide extra accommodation for thousands more spectators, there was still the dubious nature of the playing surface to consider. In particular, there were severe reservations about any building that might interfere with the all too necessary drying action of the wind. In January 1923, architect and land agent G H Sample was asked for an opinion as to the effects of a diminished airflow across the playing area if double-decker stands were to be built. What he suggested was uncovered seats at the open corners of the ground, except at the south-west, an extra row of seats installed 12 feet from the touchline and a few additional steps added at the back of the existing north and south terraces.

Another architect, Mr Styche, proposed a similar course of action, but in the opinion of Humphreys's representative, Mr Freeman, a man with 'wide experience in erecting stands', these measures were not only very costly, but they also provided comparatively very little extra seating. Freeman strongly advocated double-decking the north and south terraces to provide undercover standing below and roofed seating above, which would not only hugely increase capacity, but also revenue. In winning the day, Freeman's plans were approved together with a complete drainage programme for the pitch, which was now in a seriously deteriorated state. In all, the Union was looking at estimated costs in excess of £33,000.

This was crunch time for Twickenham. The Rugby Football Union was faced with a stark choice. Either it invested heavily in a ground patently problematical or it cut and run. Without both the capital and the commitment, the whole question of Twickenham's future was put on hold as the ground committee was charged with the task of seeking out alternative sites. Ironically, the man leading this investigation was none other than the chief architect of the dilemma, William Cail. Also, this was a post-war Britain and the timing could not have been worse.

The expansion of London at the turn of the last century is widely perceived as one of the most remarkable events in 20th century history. Increasingly, house building ate into millions of acres of green fields predominantly north and west of the capital. As the tentacles of London's Underground railway system pushed out ever further, they acted as a magnet for the house builder, intent after the Great War to create a land 'fit for heroes to live in'. Equally unhelpful to the RFU's ambitions was that whereas between 1904 and 1914 building costs had been no higher than they had been 30 years previously, by the 1920s they had escalated by more than 50 per cent.

The government selected the Wembley Park Leisure Ground in its plans for a British Empire Exhibition with a national sports stadium as its centrepiece. Wembley Stadium took just 300 days to complete at a cost of £750,000 and was opened by King George V on 23rd April 1923. Five months later, William Cail's new ground committee ended its review on the future of Twickenham. The estimated costs of alternative sites together with their respective advantages and disadvantages came in at a more modest £80,000–£100,000, but still far beyond the RFU's limited purse strings. So it was decided that the 'Great Experiment' at Twickenham would continue.

Instead of Mr Freeman's bold double-decker stands, it was decided to build a North Stand to accommodate 3,582 spectators with extensions to the existing enclosures and terraces for an additional 13,000. But even this was not without its problems. For as the popularity of Twickenham rugby ground was increasing, so too were the concerns of neighbouring district councils, transport companies, residents' associations and even the Commissioner of the Metropolitan Police.

The key to linking Twickenham with Hounslow, Southall and all towns west was Chase Bridge, spanning the Duke of Northumberland's river on the Whitton Road. Both the bridge and the river were owned and maintained by the Duke of Northumberland's estate at Syon Park. Therefore, no works or improvements could be carried out to either without the express permission of Earl Percy. Since permissions sought for more than half a century were rarely forthcoming, the narrow, 18th century, humpbacked bridge remained instrumental in restraining Whitton's road development.

The impact the ground was having outside of the game of rugby meant that proper transport links became an imperative. A halt at Whitton was refused as the railway company looked to a static population numbering less than two thousand, spread mostly about the rural village of Whitton. In 1912, the Central London Railway Company had wanted to extend their underground system beyond Richmond and, recognising the huge benefits, the Thames Valley Councils Association looked to all the local authorities affected to declare their support for the scheme.

Four hundred influential Twickenham residents, ratepayers and property owners signed a petition recording their dissatisfaction 'with the present inadequate and expensive railway service' and cordially welcomed 'increased and improved facilities'. Incredibly, the council declined to support the scheme and so the underground system never got to Twickenham. Remarkably, no dialogue, opinion or support was forthcoming from the Rugby Football Union. The only record of business with Twickenham Council at this time was an application for additional lavatory accommodation at the ground.

In 1913 the London General Omnibus Company did consider using a new type of single-decker bus that could manage Whitton's medieval road system, but with the paucity of potential passengers along the route it was felt the service would not pay. After the Great War it was a different matter. Gaps left by pre-war housing speculators were utilized to build local authority accommodation, thus increasing the population sufficiently to warrant a change of heart on the part of the bus company. On Wednesday 4th May 1921, the first omnibus passed through Whitton village from Hounslow bus depot, passing Twickenham rugby ground en route to Highgate.

Steam-driven cars had yet to fully give way to the internal combustion engine; indeed the first petrol station was not built in Britain until the 1920s, when the number of cars on the road rose from 77,000 to more than one million. Even though the RFU had early on looked to accommodate a maximum of 700 vehicles at Twickenham, rugby-loving car drivers quickly began to choke the inadequate roads serving the ground. On one occasion it took the co-operation of a prominent local resident, ex-King Manoel of Portugal, for traffic to be diverted across his fields. With the acquisition of a seven-acre piece of land, the West Motor Park was started. But so excessive were the charges for levelling and stubbing the old apple trees, that Charles Marriott took to his horse to supervise the work himself. Alf Wright recalled Marriott as a very large man. So much so that when he bestrode the poor beast, 'it went down a long way in the middle'.

For as long as anyone can remember, the grassed open space on the corner of Rugby Road and Whitton Road (sometimes referred to as 'The Front Lawn') has remained vacant, except for corporate hospitality tents. Originally it contained the most substantial house and garden on Whitton Road, dating back to the 18th century. Before 1896 it was known as 'The Laurels', then sometime after it became 'Vanda Lodge'. It was acquired by the RFU before 1923 when it was again renamed 'Rugby House' and destined to become the first 'tied' residence for RFU and retired personnel.

Transmogrified yet again, this time into 'Rugby Lodge,' the house originally earmarked for Assistant Secretary, Jack Langley, was found to be in such a poor state of repair that it was demolished. A new Rugby Lodge was built two years later, which survives (at the time of writing) as 216 Whitton Road. Immediately north of its predecessor and running parallel with Oak Lane (now Rugby Road) was a 1.5-acre orchard, which was 'slashed asunder' to create an east car park.

While charabancs and buses were banned from using the car parks at this time, maps were appearing in the London papers showing the new 'Motor Parks' at the west and east sides of the rugby ground, indicating all the 'Motor entrances'. The Wolseley Car Company placed advertisements next to these maps extolling the virtues of their 11/22 h.p. open tourer, claiming it to be: 'Just the thing for tootling off to Twickers clad in one's "Tweed Sports Suit of Jacket and Plus Four Knickers (price 59s. 6d.)" advertised by the Army & Navy Co-operative Society Ltd'.

Overall, by 1925 little had changed since the ground first opened 18 years earlier. Rugby Road, Whitton Dene and Worton Road awaited transformation from country lanes into suburban roads. Mogden Purification Works was yet to dominate the northern horizon, Tesco yet to fill the orchard space to the north-east, and what was to become known as the 'Twickenham Look' was waiting in the wings. With a record crowd of 43,000 attending the Calcutta Cup match in March 1924, the deepened rows of ringside benches were already proving inadequate. The push was on for increased accommodation as a matter of urgency.

Chapter Six

THE TWICKENHAM LOOK

'The Twickenham Look' harks back to the days when the ground comprised two great barns east and west of the pitch, a shed at the north end and a huge concrete raft at the south. That this blend of architectural styles came about in the complete absence of any real attempt at design was by no means unique to Twickenham. The design of a football ground is basically a matter of filling the space left available once the pitch has been marked out.

Open terracing is the cheapest and most spacious solution for a football ground, except where seating, which takes up a lot of space, is required. The grandstand came about as an enlarged version of the pavilion, which itself began as a wooden structure on the halfway line until it gradually stretched along the entire length of the pitch. Then, with changing rooms, tea rooms and offices to consider, the idea of putting all of these elements under one roof made good sense. Where clubs did not have sufficient space for high banking, they built two grandstands on either side with small open terraces at each end. The next stage was to concrete the terraces and provide a roof.

The *Architects' Journal* for February 1926 makes it clear that football grounds in Britain were built as 'purely functional structures', whereas in the United

States, great monuments such as the Cleveland Municipal Stadium or the Los Angeles Coliseum were built to celebrate sport. These grand arenas went beyond anything seen in Britain where the concept of design as an element of football ground construction is generally thought to belong to later 20th-century thinking when aesthetic requirements took over from traditional purely technical concerns.

While no British architect associated with British football ground construction has ever become a household name, long before 1926 there was one eminent practitioner in this niche market whose work is hugely familiar to millions of football supporters of both codes, but whose name remains largely lost to history.

Born in Glasgow in 1866, Archibald Leitch began his working life at sea as an engineer. In 1890 he obtained his Board of Trade certificate and became a superintendent draughtsman. Having set up his own company, Leitch was elected a Member of the Institute of Mechanical Engineers, going on to become a consulting mechanical engineer before turning his attention to football stadium design in 1902.

After gaining experience at various grounds in Scotland, including Hampden Park, Leitch concentrated on work south of the border. As well as Stamford Bridge, he was also responsible for the design of Ewood Park and some redevelopment of White Hart Lane, culminating just before the First World War in the layout of Arsenal's new ground at Highbury. It was at these grounds that what became known as the 'Leitch formula' was born.

This comprised essentially an ornamented full-length, two-tier grandstand on one side of the pitch, with open terracing on the other three sides.

Leitch designed the country's first double-decker stand in 1909, which comprised a seating tier above part of the terrace that enabled more spectators to be accommodated in less space. The formula was perfected when grandstand construction reached its zenith in 1922 with Aston Villa adopting a Leitch design for elegant brickwork gables, pedimented towers and stained glass.

Four years later, Leitch built Everton's Bullens Road Stand at a cost of £30,000, and three years after that he topped his career with the opening of his most ambitious construction at Ibrox Stadium, boasting a castellated press box high up in the roof as at Hampden. With its simpler and lighter criss-cross balcony built on a shelf of terracing to make it much higher and far more imposing, the stand at Highbury was Leitch's most expensive work at £60,000. In 1936, aged 70, Leitch played out his career at Roker Park and with the East Stand at White Hart Lane. Three years later, in the spring of 1939, the most prolific builder of British stadium architecture was dead. In tribute to him, when Plymouth Argyle rebuilt bombed-out Home Park in the 1950s, they recreated a Leitch double-decker.

Leitch also designed, improved or built grandstands at Leeds Road, Tynecastle Stadium, Douglas Park (Hamilton), Cardiff Arms Park, Fratton Park and Selhurst Park. The Aston Villa masterpiece survived until 2001, but all that remains today of Leitch's work is the Stevenage Road stand at Fulham's Craven Cottage. Built in 1905 and complete with its mock Tudor gable it is the only listed piece of Edwardian football stadium architecture.

Even in the 1920s, the Twickenham ground would not disgrace many a lower division football club today. Complementing its East and West Stands was a South Terrace in the form of a concrete raft built on the original ash mound and constructed shortly after the First World War. It was complete with a clock tower similar to the one at Murrayfield and under this imposing timepiece was said to abide the real spirit of Twickenham. Generations of players, young and old, would congregate here to discuss, debate and disagree. The North End still comprised mostly a low mound with limited accommodation, and it was here that the second element of the 'Twickenham Look' would be created in the form of a North Stand.

A double-decker stand was a major investment and the Union was still unconvinced about the long-term future of the ground. In opting for something less ambitious, William Cail proposed a classic two-tier stand, which provided for seats at the back and a small standing enclosure in front. It would be topped with a conventional pitched roof devoid of any adornments. The new stand would provide for an increased capacity of 10,643 in the form of 3,515 new covered reserved seats, 4,800 new covered standing, as well as 2,328 new uncovered standing on the terraces at either side of ground.

On being granted the authority to proceed, the ground committee, chaired by Cail, met with Archibald Leitch at the Great Northern Hotel on 23rd May 1924 to agree his estimate of £15,000 for such a stand. Four tenders for the work were received from Messrs Humphreys, Thorne, Ford and Walton and Trollope and Colls. The time span for completion varied from Humphreys's 20 weeks to Trollope and Colls' 38 weeks, at £19,337 and £21,877 respectively. Additional terracing work came in at between £1,977 over 12 weeks to £2,420 over 18 weeks. This meant that even

Humphreys's keen pricing came in at more than £6,000 over Leitch's original estimate, which did little to settle some serious misgivings about what repercussions such expenditure might have on member clubs and the Union's responsibilities to them.

Since the earliest days, concern was expressed that the building of a ground for the Rugby Union should not be at the expense of those who funded it. This found little sympathy with the Union's thrusting Honorary Treasurer. With around £23,000 already on loan, William Cail engineered an immediate freeze on any further requests for financial assistance and Humphreys's tender was pushed through. Even as the costs rose, Cail made no effort to rein them in, preferring instead to expand discussions with Archibald Leitch about the fate of the scoreboard, an entrance gate for the new motor park and more lavatory accommodation.

Then, in a brief note contained in the Ground Committee minutes for Friday 29th August 1924, William Cail, 'previously chair as Honorary Treasurer resigned' and was replaced by former RFU President, Ernest Prescott. Owen states that Cail retired at this time, which he did not. He remained an active member of the Finance and Emergency Committee for a few more years to come. Cail's chief cohort, the formidable Charles Marriott, was also despatched to 'expend some more of his vitality in the City' and was replaced by Engineer-Commander S F Coopper RN (Ret.), the third professional secretary of the RFU and described by Owen as 'one of the makers of modern Twickenham'.

William Cail had been in continuous office for 36 years. Backed by Marriott as Secretary and Ground Manager since 1908, he had effectively dominated the decision-making process at Twickenham. Owen records that their joint departure allowed for a new period of development. In his 1925 revision of the Rev Frank Marshall's *Football – The Rugby Union Game*, Leonard Treswill is more magnanimous, describing the 'dour, silent and impregnable' Cail as 'a staunch friend to those fortunate enough to secure his friendship'. While on the one hand he was vilified as a man 'careless of popularity', on the other there would have been no Twickenham had it not been for him. All the more poignant then, that a few hours following his departure, Archibald Leitch presented and explained the details of a prepared Plan B.

With Cail consigned to history and the completion date for the work agreed for 31st October, the committee then made a tour of the ground with Archibald Leitch. On Friday 12th September 1924, the stadium engineer issued his revised estimate for covered seats in the new North Stand at £3,582; Stand enclosures at £2,828 and North and South Terraces at £6,590. The grand total of £13,000 was a reduction of £2,000 on his original estimate. A month later he submitted a detailed plan of the new North Stand seating, which was approved. The testing of the stand was to be arranged by Leitch himself before tickets were issued for the first international of the 1924-5 season where, on 3rd January 1925, England were to meet the All Blacks for the first time since 1905.

The likelihood of any one of the 10,500 seats remaining empty was slim. These being the days before all-ticket matches, it was a matter of first come first served. The resultant fervour at the Twickenham turnstiles was exacerbated by the arrival of 'hordes of Scottish rugby fans' denied the opportunity of seeing the All Blacks in action due to rugby politics at home. The Welsh too made the long journey to see if England could emulate Wales who had put paid to the 1905 All Blacks' unbeaten record.

Even a contingent of English expats living in Paris crossed the channel to witness this, the biggest draw on the fixture list. *The Times* reported half a dozen enthusiasts ('including girls') had arrived outside Twickenham in the small hours of the morning. By ten o'clock the numbers had swelled to 5,000. In the event, stewards were instructed to 'refuse any lady or obvious non-player to occupy a player's seat'.

With Edward, Prince of Wales, Prime Minister Stanley Baldwin and other dignitaries firmly established in the comfort of the Royal Box and just eight minutes after the 2.30 kick-off, the game found a famous place in rugby history, courtesy of the All Blacks second-row forward Cyril Brownlie who was warned more than once by referee Alfred Freethy about the aggressiveness of the two sets of forwards. Brownlie ultimately paid the penalty – or was unjustly penalised according to whichever hemisphere you inhabit – and was sent off to the astonishment of the packed ground. The game resumed to see England lose a close and exciting encounter 11-17.

A massive 60,000 crowd comprehensively smashed the existing record of 43,000 established the previous season when England met Scotland, and was the largest number of people ever assembled to watch a game of rugby in the history of the game. Irrespective of Cail's cavalier methodology, the job was done and the writing was on the wall to maintain a permanent home for the England game at Twickenham.

Exactly when the North Stand was fully completed is not recorded. As ever, the RFU did not indulge in the celebratory nature of its stadium's development.

The Times in its fulsome reporting of the England v New Zealand encounter did, however, praise the recently enlarged accommodation 'by the addition of ringside seats and more spacious north and south terracing'. Discussions about the necessity for ventilation doors at the back of the 'North Terrace' were still taking place by April (1925). These large wooden shutters could be kept open when the ground was not in use so as to maintain the flow of drying air across the playing area. The North Stand as part of the Twickenham 'look' for the next 60 years was probably completed during the summer of 1925.

Throughout that summer various improvements were carried out, including mains water to replace the wind-pump. Limited electric lighting replaced the oil lamps planted throughout the stands and some additional seating was added at the front of the East and West Stands. The following year, the Middlesex Sevens came to Twickenham as the last fixture of the season. Mainly a fun day before the summer months, the story is told that in 1882 the Melrose club in the Scottish Borders fell into financial difficulties. A local butcher who was a member of the club had the idea of staging an inter-club tournament in which teams of seven apiece would play a modified form of rugby.

English and Welsh clubs flocked to take part in what became an annual tournament organised by Melrose, Galashiels and Hawick. It was brought south by a Scotsman, Dr Jimmy Russell-Cargill, then a member of the Middlesex Committee and later president of the RFU – hence the name of the cup presented to the winners at the end of the day. Fifty clubs entered for the first tournament in 1926, which was won by Harlequins, as were the next three. London Welsh managed to break the spell. Just as it was doing for the national game, so Twickenham was proving as much a lucky talisman for its tenant.

In 1927 it was generally agreed that the time was 'seriously ripe' to consider building a stand at the south end of the ground in order to increase capacity. By no means for the first time in the ground's history, serious concerns were expressed about keeping the pitch 'free and open to air and sun'. Whereas a north/south alignment allows for maximum daylight to the playing surface throughout the year, a stand at the south end, it was feared, would create shadows, which in turn would retard the growth of half the pitch.

The preferred option was to add another twenty steps to the existing concrete slab backwards and upwards to accommodate 5,000 spectators. Once the work was completed, it was agreed that the British Broadcasting Corporation could erect a permanent platform there at its own expense, marking something of a milestone year in the annals of British broadcasting wherein the nation was fast becoming hooked on the new diversion of 'listening'.

The British Broadcasting Company was dissolved in 1926 and its shareholders paid off. During its four-year existence, the number of receiving licences had risen to two-and-a-quarter million, despite the fact that the ten-shilling (50p) fee was a substantial outlay for the majority of the population. But for the first time it was possible to listen 'live' to commentaries on events we now take for granted from the comfort of our armchairs. A microphone was first positioned on the banks of the Thames to cover the Oxford and Cambridge boat race in April 1927, but the first-ever live radio sports commentary broadcast by the newly incorporated BBC had taken place at Twickenham on 15th January that same year.

A prehistoric version of the technology-packed monsters of today, the first BBC Outside Broadcast van at Rugby HQ sat beneath a state-of-the-art wood and corrugated iron 'media centre', which housed the pioneer rugby football commentator, Teddy Wakelam. To a potential listening audience 450,000 times the size of a packed Twickenham stadium, the former Harlequin reported L S Corbett's try for England, which was converted by E Stanbury who then took a penalty kick. In reply, G E Andrews and R Harding each scored a try for Wales followed up by a penalty kick from B O Male. With customary caution, the Rugby Football Union declared that the practice of players writing articles and reports of matches was 'contrary to the spirit of Rugby football', while guidance from the BBC to its commentators was contained in the form of a short notice pinned in front of the microphone: 'Do not swear'.

Topped with the classic simplicity of Archibald Leitch's North Stand and tailed by the growing concrete raft to the south, attention soon turned to extending the original A and B stands east and west. Initially the idea was to extend back one or both about eight rows to create 1,900 extra capacity.

The preferred option, however, was to add a second deck of seating to accommodate around 5,000 extra spectators. At £20,000 per stand, this was no small investment and logistically a potential nightmare. Mindful of lost revenue, the Treasurer Ernest Prescott demanded an assurance that such work would be completed before the start of the next season's important matches.

Prudently, it was decided that only the East Stand should be extended at this time, together with work to the South Terrace. The firms of Humphreys Ltd; Guest,

Keen and Nettlefold; The Trussed Concrete Steel Co, and Braithwaite and Co; 'and these firms alone' were considered for tender, with the Union reserving the right to require and to use any design submitted, whether accepted or not. The services of a consultancy engineer, J M Kennedy, were secured to advise on the estimates and to supervise the alterations. To save time, direct authority was granted to the Ground Committee to accept the tender it considered most suitable.

Two days after an incredibly tight deadline, estimates were received from only The Trussed Concrete Steel Co and Humphreys. Both estimates came in at around £34,000 and would have been identical had The Trussed Concrete Steel Company included the £250 for re-alignment of the clock tower. But with their design deemed inferior to that of their rivals, the contract went to Messrs Humphreys Ltd.

With its second covered tier built over the original seating, the new East Stand was strikingly similar to an Archibald Leitch 'double-decker', but for an average of £10,000 less than that charged by Messrs Humphreys Ltd, his preferred construction engineers. The existing and new seating extended approximately 27 feet at each end with back rests provided for the new seats. At the rear of the original stand above the existing seating, louvred doors and windows were fitted to both reduce air pressure and to give light below the new flooring.

By December 1927, gleaming corrugated steel sheeting coated the entire structure and electric lighting was installed to the Upper Stand. The first of the great barns was now a feature on the Twickenham landscape, but was at the same time a shining beacon to the ground's continuing success and a monument to misplacement. For as the popularity of the ground increased, so too did the problems of accessing it, particularly by road.

Mostly the business of acquiring extra land for car parking was a very gradual, haphazard process encompassing all sorts of arrangements and compromises with neighbouring landowners. Many an opportunity was lost because of the Union's variable cash flow or its bouts of indecision. The worst example was in 1928 with the loss for the second time in the Union's history of the neighbouring 28-acre Erncroft Estate (now mostly the Twickenham Trading Estate off Rugby Road), which was the very land originally selected by Billy Williams in 1906 as the preferred site for the ground.

This time around, and due to Union expenditure in the region of £150,000, there was again little room for manoeuvre. Even so, the value of this extra land saw the Union keen to find a way to acquire it. Unfortunately, a decision to wait and see how proposed new road development schemes in the district would pan out saw the opportunity slip away. Secretary Coopper for one believed it was a big mistake not to buy it.

As well as an extra eighteen acres of car parking and with greatly improved access off the London Road, ten acres could have been used to create in-house practice pitches, a move which would have been welcomed by Alf Wright as putting an end to 'chasing all over London' for the use of others. The RFU would have then been completely independent and Twickenham's future a very different one. But with its substantial overdraft, the Union simply could not afford the £12,000 asking price. This was after all a time when the Great Depression had reached its nadir and the most often used word in the business press was 'retrenchment'. Today, the Union's offices at Rugby House on Rugby Road occupy a fraction of this site.

Also, as the RFU changed forever the skyline of this part of west Middlesex, Mother Nature was busy indulging in her own time-honoured tradition. In the early hours of a Tuesday morning in January 1928, just days away from the match against New South Wales, 'water rushed across the [West] car park, flooding to such a depth that a boat could have floated behind the South Terrace'. This was a disaster waiting to happen. Decades of correspondence had flowed between the local authorities and the Duke of Northumberland's estate at Syon Park about the temperamental nature of his waterway. But here again, the RFU failed to support the local authority's efforts to end this archaic state of affairs, putting instead its energies towards a suitable memorial on the flood plain to Sir George Rowland Hill, who had served as a committee member from 1879 to 1928 when he died.

As Honorary Secretary of the RFU from 1881-1904 and thrice-elected president from 1904-1907, Hill gave his backing for the purchase of the Twickenham ground. He was created a Knight Bachelor in 1926, the first to be so honoured for services to the Rugby game. In his obituary *The Times* recalled 'an amateur of amateurs and a Tory of Tories'. The Rowland Hill Memorial was decided upon to celebrate a life given to the Rugby game at home and 'throughout the empire'. Letters were received from the Scottish, Irish and Welsh Unions stating they were prepared to take part in the Opening Ceremony on 5th October 1929, with the net proceeds given to the King's Thanksgiving Fund.

The memorial was originally positioned in the generous gap between South View (182) and number 202 Whitton Road and now forms the centrepiece of the new triumphal Lion Gate leading into the ground from the west car park. Fittingly, the England team of 1929 beat Wales 8-3 in front of an official crowd of 65,000. Many of those unable to gain entry to the ground climbed trees or secured whatever other vantage points they could to add to the RFU's thoughts on extra accommodation.

Despite suffering yet another chronic cash flow, the ground's proven success year on year meant that the cost of building a new West Stand would soon recoup the investment. So an unusual Special Sub-Committee was formed comprising the President, W T Pearce, the Honorary Treasurer, Ernest Prescott and the two Vice-presidents, R F Oakes and Adrian Stoop, to oversee the work. They determined that the contract would not go out to open tender but be placed directly with Messrs Humphreys Ltd, who were by now the Union's preferred contractor.

The estimated costs had come in at slightly less than for the East Stand, with an assurance that work to the lower section of the new West Stand would be completed by 1st September 1930. Provided the order was placed in good time, the upper tier would be completed by September 1931. As well as the rearrangement of offices, dressing rooms, tearooms and 'comfort facilities', the general principles were unanimously agreed at an estimated cost of £64,000. But then a word of caution crept into the proceedings when a member of the Finance and Emergency Committee questioned the Union's not putting the work out to open tender. This presented something of a problem to the Special Committee as the previous minutes carried the motion for the tender to be placed directly with Humphreys.

Despite Messrs Humphreys's proven track record, the consulting engineer was asked to attend a special meeting to answer: (1) if the estimate for the new scheme was an economic figure; (2) if the Rugby Union was committed to place the contract with Humphreys and; (3) if work was put out to open tender would it be completed by the time stated. Mr Donkin (representing the consulting engineers) replied that his methods of checking prices and labour costs were carefully carried out to include all materials and wages, etc., and that in his opinion it was an economic proposition. Although the Union was not legally committed, Messrs Humphreys could claim a payment for work done on plans for the original scheme, but not for the new scheme, although the plans were their property.

In Donkin's view the work would most probably be delayed if put to open tender, as preparation of new plans and specifications would prevent the estimate being accepted before the new year. Also, the committee was warned, if a cut-price contract was accepted then the work would probably not be carried out so satisfactorily for all concerned. In agreeing that Messrs Humphreys should proceed on the lines indicated, included in the contract was an extra tearoom, an additional committee room, a president's room and yet more 'comfort' accommodation. The latter included two ladies' lavatories and two men's urinals under the South Terrace 'on the strict understanding that they were only to be used for their proper purpose'.

Blissfully unaware of all this, spectators in the old A stand meanwhile watched England beat France

11-5. With wins at Cardiff and Dublin doing enough to secure another championship, the Army and Navy played the last match to be viewed from the ground's remaining original vantage point on the first Saturday in March 1930. The following Monday, Alf Wright watched the workmen arrive 'with all their gear', pull down the old stand and immediately start work on the new one, which boasted a limited hot water system, primarily for the players' new changing rooms, and a radiator pipe to warm the Royal Box. Before closing in the south end of the new stand, it was decided to paint in giant white lettering 'West' on the iron sheeting and then 'East' on its opposite number.

On 17th September 1931 the local authority tested the new 23,000 capacity West Stand and approved it to be as 'amply strong enough to carry with perfect safety all the loads which might be applied to them by crowds of spectators'. Complete with a grand entrance accessed through the new Rowland Hill Memorial Gate, the whole structure, including dressing rooms, committee rooms and tea rooms was built in just seven months at a cost of £75,000. The Twickenham Look that would grace the west Middlesex skyline for the next 60 years was born.

Chapter Seven

BEYOND THE TURNSTILES

It is a fundamental expectation of major sporting stadia to act as prime motivators for land use change in the promotion of transport links and the development of other services that will attract housing to generate schools, hospitals and retail opportunities. At Twickenham however, motivation beyond its turnstiles was never a consideration. Rugby HQ's largely splendid isolation continued amidst undeveloped roads leading to and from the ground and the troublesome Duke's River.

As ever an issue for others to resolve, it was not until 1928 that the Middlesex County Council promoted a Bill in Parliament in order to acquire control of the unpredictable waterway from Earl Percy. This was acceded to under the proviso that the Bill safeguarded the rights and privileges concerning the water supply to Syon Park. In return, the Duke of Northumberland's river was contained within the concrete causeway familiar today and the narrow, humpbacked Chase Bridge was rebuilt to accommodate 20th-century traffic.

The RFU did concern itself with all the road traffic it attracted once it had made it to the ground. In 1931, to kick-start the north car park, the Union purchased six acres of ground at the corner of Whitton Dene and Rugby Road together with Clitheroe Cottages, which were added to the Union's portfolio of accommodation for RFU employees and retired staff. With the ground able to accommodate 3,000 of the vehicles that stoically made the arduous journey, there was plenty of money to be made parking them. The National Car Park Company offered to manage the new north car park complete with uniformed officials on payment of 75% of takings, but the Royal Automobile Club was chosen instead at a more competitive 15% of gross receipts.

A further one-and-a-half acres of meadow was then leased from a W D Hitchcock as an extension to the west car park, with both parties taking an equal share of the takings for a trial season. The relationship between the RFU and Mr Hitchcock stretched back at least to 1923 when the market gardener was first approached to sell a 40-foot strip of his land. This was not an attractive proposition to Mr Hitchcock, as it would have meant the removal of his mushroom house. Besides, and to the obvious chagrin of the Committee, he also stood to lose his capacity to make the not inconsiderable sum of £180 per year parking cars on match days.

The Southern Railway Company wanted to call the new station Twickenham West, which brought about a furious response from local residents who pointed out in a memorandum to the local authority that 4,000 people were now living in Whitton, and that number would soon 'double at least'. During questions by members of Twickenham council it was made plain that Whitton was where the station was located, and so Whitton it should be called. With Twickenham a good two miles away, the debate concluded that the name of Twickenham West would be confusing to people travelling to Whitton, 'especially footballers wanting to go to the rugby ground – and other strangers'.

Just as the railways in the 19th century offered escape routes from the slums and overcrowding of the towns and cities, so too did the great roads of the inter-war years. Arguably the most indicative was the Great West Road (now the A4), lined with its magnificent art deco monuments to industry, each employing armies drawn from the new semi-detached population straddling its golden route west from London. Later, the Chertsey Arterial would not only provide another fast track out of the capital and west beyond the plains of west Middlesex, but for the first time involve Twickenham Rugby Ground as a participating player on the developing landscape. As Twickenham fell to the Welsh in a 7-3 win over an inconsistent England, so it was decided to construct a new bridge over the Thames from London.

On its completion in July 1932, the Twickenham Road Bridge, 45,000 tons of concrete and 800 tons of steel, alleviated the need for the first time in history to travel through Richmond and Twickenham to reach Whitton and all towns west. When the new section of the Chertsey Road from St Margaret's roundabout was opened in time for the Varsity Match on the 12th December 1933, an end was optimistically announced to 'the crawl to Twickenham rugby matches'. Historian, Gordon S Maxwell, meanwhile gloomily walked down Oak Lane from the direction of Isleworth, passing through meadows and lanes of the 'little Middlesex hamlet of Mogden', with its one picturesque farm and 'not large enough to be called a village'.

Rugby Road was still 'but a bush-fringed lane'. Maxwell reckoned that the total population north and east of the ground did not exceed more than a dozen. As he ambled along the picturesque banks of the Duke's river 'flowing through the fields' he imagined himself one day to be quite alone and on another 'hard pressed to find space amongst the sudden insurgence of 70,000 visitors to the Rugby Football Ground at Twickenham'.

Much still remained of the former Erncroft Estate, the original site selected for the Rugby Ground, although most of it towards the London Road was being dredged of its gravel content or spotted with new housing developments. Maxwell's heart jumped a beat with the frenzied development under way towards Whitton. Clutches of new housing development flanked the new Chertsey Arterial, which was formally declared 'a Class One Motor Route' on 6th June 1937. An early build to the section of the new road was cut into Whitton Road, so as to alleviate some of the crowd problems created by the ground.

The roundabouts dotted along the Chertsey Arterial's initial limited length were at one time to be adopted as a series of 'circuses' beginning at St Margaret's and leading to Hospital Bridge. What might have become more familiar as a local landmark in the form of 'Rugby Circus' instead gave way to a roundabout synonymous with a car dealership, or 'nice people to do business with', as they once liked to put it. Rugby 'HQ' meanwhile continued to thrive, as much a part of the English sporting calendar as Lord's, Ascot or Henley. Before it was built, the Rugby Football Union was a homeless and rather nebulous body. But well within three decades, it had been transformed, complete with a stadium that was unique in its character.

The height of its stands, and the atmosphere produced on big match days prompted the French rugby correspondent, Jean Denis, to dub it 'The Cathedral of Rugby'; a view not shared by Richmond

Borough Council, which objected to the corruption of the view from Richmond Hill. This being the only view in Britain protected by an Act of Parliament, the Rugby Football Union's challenging, corrugated ironclad construction, they thought, had no place decimating the gentility of Arcadia on Thames.

In a stiff memorandum to Richmond Corporation, Commander Coopper asked if the authority had any specific proposals to make for the committee to consider. The town clerk suggested a screen of poplar trees planted in the east car park, to which the erstwhile RFU Secretary pointed out even after 50 years the planting would have 'little or no effect'. Deeply unimpressed, the town clerk wrote back regretting the RFU's attitude, stating that if the Corporation was able to bring any pressure to bear on the Union then it would do so. In the opinion of the Twickenham Ratepayers' Association the ground presented an 'unsightly appearance', and they secured the support of Richmond Corporation in asking for the steel skin of the stands to be painted green.

No trees were planted, but the stands were later painted, but not to enhance the view from Richmond Hill nor to oblige its neighbours, but to baffle the efforts of a far more sinister foe threatening the peace of the wider planet. The year 1939 marked the 50th international played at the ground with a game between England and Ireland, which saw for the first time a special police guard at Twickenham following a series of IRA bomb outrages on the mainland. The game went ahead without incident to see Ireland beat England 5-0. Later that same year, however, came the arrival of a much greater threat, wherein the Rugby Football Union swung into action for a second time that century to do its bit.

Following the declaration of war with Germany in September 1939, the RFU cancelled all rugby fixtures. A freeze was put on outstanding loans and all subscriptions and season tickets were repaid. In true RFU style, a brace of committees was instantly formed. An Emergency Committee looked after the requisitioned Twickenham ground and other corporate RFU interests, with an Inter-Services Committee taking over the arrangement and responsibility of all matches and conduct of the game across the country. This included stout stuff such as allowing for a Services Rugby XV to comprise both League and Union players.

University, Schools and Hospital matches were encouraged to carry on, and the Middlesex Sevens continued to be played unbroken at Richmond Athletic ground. Commander S F Coopper, as Secretary, and Head Groundsman Charles (Charlie) Hale were left to maintain the ground for the duration. As the other staff, players and the supporters shipped out, so the Air-Raid Precaution (ARP) volunteers and the hospital authorities marched in. Twickenham was requisitioned as a civil defence depot, with special responsibilities as a decontamination centre in the event of a chemical attack on London.

The dressing rooms were stripped for the installation of anti-gas equipment and the east car park was dug up as part of the 'Dig For Victory' campaign. An air raid shelter was sunk at the south end of the East Stand and the west car park was split between the demands of the National Fire Service for the storage of its heavy vehicles, while the north end became a coal dump. The dank, gloomy confines under the South Terrace were given over as a fire guard centre and for the storage of national fire service pumps and appliances.

In place of supporters, sack loads of salvaged materials filled the terrace of Archibald Leitch's North Stand, while surgical instruments replaced the clink of cutlery in the West Stand restaurant, which had been transformed into a first aid post, sick bay and casualty receiving station. Women clad in blue serge replaced the tweed and cloth of the Rugby Football Union committee members as their tearoom gave way to the ladies' rest room. The only things spared were the Secretary's offices and the pitch.

Evidence that the conflict was near its end came days after the war in Europe ended. The Rugby Football Union held its first post-war Annual General Meeting at the Mayfair Hotel on 22nd June 1945 where before business a minute's silence was called in tribute to all the rugby football players who had lost their lives in the conflict. Appreciation was also expressed to all of those whom, despite intensive bombing, threats of invasion, food, transport and clothing difficulties, kept the game alive to play its part in maintaining the country's morale.

Coopper particularly was singled out for praise in making it possible for clubs throughout Britain to obtain the necessary coupons for football jerseys, and certificates for balls and bladders. Coopper was seen as the man who against great odds had maintained 'HQ' throughout the war years. Also, he had earned the huge respect of the various wartime agencies billeted at Twickenham due to his courtesy and helpfulness shown throughout.

Although due for retirement, the army retained Coopper's replacement, Colonel F D Prentice, who was due to start in the summer of 1946. This was in fact good news for Twickenham. Sydney Coopper had been Secretary for so many years that he knew the ground like the back of his hand and was therefore best placed to ensure that it reverted back to its intended use sooner rather than later with an unprecedented force of ten salaried staff, including the first woman employee in the form of office secretary, Mrs Potts.

The closest the ground got to being hit by enemy action was in July 1944 when a V1 flying bomb fell in the front garden of 17 Talma Gardens opposite the West Gate, injuring sixteen people. Anti-aircraft shell splinters had damaged the stand roofs, but by far the worst effects of the war came from the sheer lack of maintenance. The upper deck of the West Stand especially could not be used in wet weather or in high winds.

The job of recovery was no mean task, for organisations such as the RFU found themselves way down the food chain when it came to obtaining the necessary labour licences. Top priority was afforded the rebuilding of the nation's war-torn infrastructure and especially housing. But a nation starved of sport during the war years was champing at the bit to file through the turnstiles, so it was down to RFU staff to undertake repairs as best they could in between fixtures, which they did.

Despite the seriously poor condition of the West Stand's upper deck, the first post-war game at Twickenham took place on 24th November 1945, when an England XV took on the New Zealand Army Touring Side, entertaining a crowd of 27,300. The home team was roundly beaten 18-3, but did manage to score a victory over Ireland (14-6) the following February. A return encounter with Wales brought defeat by a try to nothing, and Scotland was beaten 12-8.

Later in the year a licence was obtained from the Ministry of Works for expenditure of £3,336 for essential works, of which about £2,000 was recoverable from the War Damage Commission for repairs to the West Stand. A £12,000 claim for damages caused during requisitioning was reduced to £7,000 and strictly confined to repairing those parts of the property actually occupied. The Rowland Hill Memorial survived. Its gates had been removed and the twin stiles packed with boxes of sand for protection. But the area underneath the South Terrace had become seriously neglected and was infested by rats. The space had been used for cutting up logs to supplement fuel, which, like every other commodity at the time was in short supply.

Chapter Eight

HALF-TIME

The Services Tournament and the Middlesex Sevens returned to a sad-looking Twickenham in 1946. The following year, the King and Queen, accompanied by Princess Elizabeth, were among a record crowd of more than 40,000 to watch the University Match, which was played for the first time on a Saturday, partly on appeal from the government for sport not to break into the working week during the current economic crisis.

For their part, the RFU readily agreed, thinking that it might build on the record crowd if the game was always played on a Saturday. As it happened, fewer than 4,000 spectators turned up the following year, so the idea was not repeated. A year later, back on a Tuesday, the record for a University Match was again smashed with 59,400 in attendance.

Off the field of play, Sydney Coopper achieved what he had set out to do. Twickenham was back in business and well on the road to full recovery. On the occasion of his retirement after 24 years, Engineer Commander S F Coopper RN (Ret.) was described as 'the Founder of Modern Twickenham'. As such, the inevitable handing over of power to Colonel Prentice was seen as 'a delicate matter'.

Frank Prentice played for England in 1928 and captained the British Lions team to New Zealand and Australia in 1930 and was one of a team of five selectors up to the outbreak of war in 1939. His twin sons frequently accompanied him on his visits to Twickenham each season and invariably stayed for tea with the Cooppers at South View, never once imagining that one day their father would become RFU Secretary and that they would occupy the fine old house.

In 1948, one of the sons, Tom, returned from India and helped in the old RFU office in the West Stand packing batches of tickets to be sent to the major clubs. His memories are of everything in short supply and the ground still requiring much repair work to be done. The stand roofs were still holed by stray shrapnel. The steelwork was rusty, the crowd barriers weakened and seats in need of repair or replacement. But at least the Twickenham magic was still there, if not always for the host side.

The year 1948 was an excellent one for the Irish, scoring more tries than they had done in a championship season in 20 years and squeaking a win by one point (11-10) at Twickenham. Thus far, William Cail's grand gesture had more than repaid the Union's trust in his scheme. The thought of a rugby world without its Twickenham was akin to imagining tennis without Wimbledon, cricket without Lord's or racing without Ascot. The Grande Dame of Rugby Union had come of age, but unfortunately she was starting to show it.

In the last year that spectators could pay through the turnstiles, it is uncertain exactly how many got into the ground for 1950's England v Wales encounter. Thousands arrived only to discover all the tickets had been sold, which led to many gaining entry to the ground whichever way they could. A reading had to be taken of every turnstile at the end of each match to be submitted to the Inland Revenue in compliance with the Entertainment Duty Tax. This showed a record-breaking attendance of over 75,532 witnesses to an English defeat at the hands of the Welsh visitors by 11-5.

Counting machines were also installed to record the numbers of spectators in each enclosure, except to the South Terrace where there was standing only, thus no seat numbers on tickets. Here, it was discovered, were always far more spectators than tickets issued. Following a check, it was found 'on a frighteningly dangerous scale' that some of the uniformed agency gatekeepers were accepting ten-shilling notes in lieu. Newly appointed Honorary Treasurer, William 'Bill' Ramsay then suggested the idea of replacing the South Terrace with a stand.

To achieve this meant lopping off the gardens to the neighbouring houses in Whitton Road, only one of which at that time was owned by the Union. Unless arrangements could be made with all of the owners, this meant that all the houses would have to be acquired. Ramsay felt that such a scheme would be too expensive, believing that the Union's finances were better utilised supporting clubs and so the idea was dropped. Instead, the much-loved clock tower was torn down to make way for what was to become another iconic feature on the stadium landscape.

Designed by Kenneth Dalgleish in 1949 and built by Messrs Comyn Ching and Co, for £165, the famous weathervane made its debut at HQ in 1950. Resplendent with bronze lettering and depicting a near life-sized figure of Hermes, the messenger of the gods, passing a rugby ball to a modern youth in full stride beneath a set of goalposts, it became a symbol of Twickenham on television for many years and (at the time of writing) is affixed to the southern end of the East Stand.

The winter of 1951-2 was one of the coldest on record. Some 20 tons of straw was used to protect the pitch from the severe frosts, thus enabling 64,000 spectators to watch England lose to the fourth Springboks 3-8, but beat Ireland 3-0 in blizzard conditions. Access to the ground by rail was improved with the replacement of Twickenham's characterful Victorian railway station by a typically bland, functional post-war box on the east side of London Road. Aesthetics aside, the new facility did include the doubling of the number of platforms as well as one specifically for use on rugby days. Legend has it that the RFU paid for this additional facility, although its benevolence is not officially celebrated in minute books or elsewhere.

In 1953 England claimed their first championship since 1947, drawing with Ireland and beating Wales and Scotland. A satisfying 11-0 win over France added to a sunny winter's day at HQ. A year later, and following an 8-3 victory for Wales at Twickenham, England won the Grand Slam and received its first wake-up call as to the condition of its home when settlement problems were reported under the north and south terrace areas. This meant their closure for extensive works to be carried out while England went to Paris to lose to France (3-11), but win against Scotland at Murrayfield (13-3).

The upper drift of the South Terrace also required renovation, including a means of waterproofing the creaking concrete platform. By mid-July, repairs to the north and south terrace areas were virtually finished and work began on building a bar, a luncheon room and ground staff accommodation under the South Terrace. However, when it came to waterproofing its enormous concrete underbelly, huge cracks were discovered in the slab caused by the steel skeleton's joints bulging with rust. What remedial work could be done was carried out.

There was no immediate danger to spectators for the coming season, but as it stood, the South Terrace represented recurring and increasing heavy annual expenditure. The Ground Committee minutes for 21st February 1957 express little doubt that ultimately the whole concrete raft would require replacing at an estimated cost of more than £40,000. The preferred solution was for a new stand to be built over the existing terracing, which would increase capacity by a further 4,000 seats.

Meanwhile, the underside was painted as an additional sealer against damp, and the concrete steps were repaired in time for Twickenham's Jubilee Season, 1959-60. The main highlight of the season was a match played on 17th October 1959 in tribute to the very first match played on Billy Williams's Cabbage Patch between Harlequins and Richmond. Seven of the original Harlequins players assembled for a group photograph with their counterparts 50 years on. Sadly missing from the line-up was one of Twickenham's favourite sons, A D (Adrian) Stoop, who had died two years earlier.

U A Tilley and Ross McWhirter include in their *Centenary History of the Rugby Football Union* an unaccredited tribute to the legendary figure: 'In the development of attacking rugby, in the technique and act of passing and running, and especially for the part he played in establishing the stand-off as the vital part of the attack, he will stand among the greatest of all time in the history of Rugby Football.' Adrian Stoop was also a prime mover in the success of Twickenham Rugby Ground. Without his personal contribution and that of his Harlequins club as the added attraction to an otherwise unattractive and inaccessible venue, it is doubtful whether the stadium would have thrived as it has.

As Captain, Secretary and President of Harlequins and then Captain of England and later President of the Rugby Football Union, Stoop's record remains unequalled and his name is immortalised at The Stoop Memorial Ground, the home today of Harlequins Football Club.

Twenty-three returning British Lions took part in the Jubilee match between England and Wales v Scotland and Ireland. England and Wales won by 26-17, with ten tries to thrill the spectators. In the evening 3,000 guests were entertained in two tents set up in the west car park in aid of the Rugby Football Union Charitable Trust. In the championship, Ken Scotland levelled the score with England for his namesake nation 3-3.

The sixties swung into action with England enjoying a convincing 14-6 win over Wales. With France on a mighty roll, but England managing to force a 5-5 draw on home turf, Twickenham's continued popularity forced the RFU to consider a new, dynamic statement that would take the stadium forward. The obvious candidate was the redevelopment of the sickly South Terrace.

In June 1964, the architectural firm of Sir Owen Williams and Partners put forward a design for a partially prefabricated cantilevered stand that provided for additional seating over the South Terrace. Supported by eight central pillars, which in turn housed service lifts and staircases as a separate unit, the structure offered 90 per cent cover for the existing terrace. With 11,500 seats or 10,000 seats and 3,000 extra standing, plus ancillary buffets and bars, the new seating accommodation was designed to provide for two inches extra leg room and wider seating with arm rests of nineteen inches. The cost based on £20 per seat was estimated at around £225,000.

As the Irish condemned England to an 18-5 defeat, further design modifications looked to bring the proposed structure considerably closer to the pitch. Although 4,000 standing places were lost at the rear, 9,500 spectators were presented with an almost unrestricted view, with the front seats enjoying the same view as those in the North Stand. It would be constructed of concrete, aluminium and glass, with all exposed steelwork enclosed to reduce maintenance; space was made available for offices and small meeting rooms.

The original design included what looked to some like four 'chimneys' poking out from the structure when viewed from the south. These were removed from the plans and, with precious little thought given to wider public consultation, work was planned to start the following summer. The chaps at HQ were raring to go. With the outline proposals accepted, Sir Owen Williams and Partners duly applied for planning permission. But then, much to their horror and surprise, they found their application refused on four counts. Three objections centred on the houses occupying the north side of Whitton Road. By 'the nature of its height and bulk', the proposed structure was felt to be unduly obtrusive and prejudicial to the enjoyment of these properties by their occupants. The other objection focused on the lack of additional car parking required to accommodate the increased capacity.

Such was the phenomenal growth in car ownership after the war, coupled with poor public transport links, getting to the ground by car had become a favoured option. So troublesome had the question of parking become that elaborate schemes had had to be introduced by the police. In its defence, the RFU was able to put forward a recently signed agreement and £12,000 ploughed into creating space at Harlequins' new Craneford Way Stadium, which they had acquired as a training ground in 1963 and moved to shortly afterwards. And having lost out on thirteen acres of land north of the ground to a building company, serious thought had been given to double-decking the west car park. All of this demonstrated that the Union was aware of car parking as an issue over time, but it cut no ice with the authorities.

Forty members of Twickenham Council rejected the new 160ft high, 350ft long proposed South Stand. Harking back to an earlier, unresolved grievance, a letter received from Richmond Corporation declared its opposition on the grounds that the structure was 'too massive' and would 'impair the view from Richmond Hill'. Remarkably, just a single opinion was expressed in the *Richmond and Twickenham Times* letters page, ostensibly on behalf of the entire local community, declaring that 'the adding of a few feet to the height of a stand was a small price to pay compared to the rise in prosperity to the borough in increased revenue'.

After all, the correspondent added, other boroughs had resolved similar parking problems, why not Twickenham? As for the height of the new stand, he reckoned that the sun would have to be very low in the sky before it denied light to the gardens of the six houses abutting the proposed stand. Moreover, Twickenham, as the Mecca of the Rugby World, enjoyed a unique position both at home and overseas.

At this time Twickenham Borough was being

merged into a newly created London Borough of Richmond upon Thames. Possibly the RFU thought the scheme would somehow slide through the air of quiet depression, as committee members were urged to go forth and make every effort to lobby council members and especially the borough engineer. The crowd packing the South Terrace watching Andy Hancock run his famous ninety metres for a try against Scotland, thus denying them their first win at Twickenham since 1938, was blissfully unaware of the politics beneath their feet as a furious RFU looked to a public enquiry.

The Minister for Housing and Local Government's decision was taken without prejudice to a further application being made should the RFU acquire three of the houses adjacent to its southern border that it did not own. In this, the Union was required to authorise a Twickenham estate agent to value the houses and to negotiate on its behalf with £500 added for disturbance, and £100 towards any costs incurred. Once achieved, the Union could re-apply to the ministry. This effectively rocketed the RFU right back to square one in so far as one of the major drawbacks in the choice of site was that it did not adjoin Whitton Road.

Eight detached Victorian villas originally ran the length of the site's southern boundary, with a narrow access way dividing them from a stretch of 'new' Edwardian houses to the west. This was the reason why Twickenham could not enjoy a grand, impressive entrance. Other entrances and exits off Whitton Road only came about over time as the Union acquired some of these properties. Rugby Lodge (number 216) was built by the RFU in 1925 as accommodation for Assistant Secretary Langley.

In that same year, 'South View' (182) was purchased

at the suggestion of William Cail. The owner, Mr Styche, was one of the legion of architects employed by the Union over time, who doubtless saw the writing on the wall as far as the long-term view from his kitchen window was concerned. Purchased for £2,100, 'South View' was earmarked as the residence of RFU secretary Sydney Coopper at an annual rent of £50.

What remains (at the time of writing) of an impressive garden attaching South View was once considered for use as a car park for committee members, but this was declined in favour of a 'more dignified Main Entrance to the ground'. The five other houses have each fluctuated in value according to the fortunes of the stadium. In 1934 Oakley Lodge (178) was purchased by the RFU and torn down to make way for a new ticket gate.

This left 'Roseham' (176) neighbouring one side of the new thoroughfare and 'Headthorpe' (180) the other. Sensing its value to the RFU, when Roseham first came up for sale in the 1930s, the RFU had to arrange for a third party to make enquiries to ensure the lowest price. Twenty-five years later, it was finally purchased for less than half the asking price. 'Holmwood Lodge' (now 170 Whitton Road) was acquired at the same time for staff accommodation.

In January 1967 a letter was sent to the Minister of Housing and Local Government asking that the RFU's planning application be reconsidered after approaches had been made to the householders. The following April, the RFU solicitors were instructed to accept the 'inflated asking prices' for as many of the houses along the north side of Whitton Road as were available. The Union was hungry for them and the owners knew it. Number 180 occupied a prime site, sandwiched

between South View and Ticket Gate No. 4. Valued at
£8,250, it was purchased by the RFU for a staggering
£13,000. Number 220 was also conveniently situated
alongside No. 2 Car Park Gate. Here the tenants were
approached to buy the house and then resell it to the
Union, but refused.

Further along the road, number 226 was purchased
for £4,750, but at number 208, which was closer to the
ground, the owner wanted £6,500. By August 1967, the
three properties stymieing the proposed South Stand
project were purchased and a further application for
planning was lodged. If satisfied, work was planned
to start in April 1968 for completion in August 1970.
The plan was then to purchase number 220 Whitton
Road and demolish it along with Rugby Lodge to
treble the width of Car Park Gate No. 2.

Numbers 172-182 would also be demolished along
with number 202 on the other side of the Rowland
Hill Entrance No. 3. This just left numbers 172 and
174, which, when eventually purchased, would also
be torn down to open up the whole of the area directly
abutting the South Terrace. Other, less strategic,
properties would be purchased on an ad hoc basis
towards an even more ambitious future.

Rampant with the same optimism as his predecessor, William Cail, 60 years earlier, the Honorary
Treasurer, Bill Ramsay, then set about entering the
Union into an agreement with the GLC (as the
planning authority) intended to lead to permission
for the new South Stand. In January 1968, Ramsay
confirmed that sufficient funds were available and
planning permission for the new 10,753 capacity
stand would be granted the day that the six houses
were vacated. The trustees agreed that as soon
as permission was received, a meeting should be

arranged with the consulting engineers to short-list firms for tender; but then, disaster.

The quantity surveyor's probable cost came in at £430,000, or just less than double the original estimate. As well as this, the whole of the South Terrace area would have to be sterilized for seventeen months with a further £70,000 found to cover other costs and expenses. This massive hike came as an expensive 'surprise' to Ramsay, causing him to reconsider the whole proposition. Satisfied that a maximum ceiling of £400,000 could be raised and repaid over seven years, the whole package was referred to the AGM in the hope that even if the scheme exceeded £410,000 it would still proceed. That is until concerns were expressed about the tight timescale, possible hold-ups due to bad weather or labour disputes and subsequent effects on the rugby programme.

When the selected contractors, George Wimpey and Co, dropped in their estimate for a completely unexpected £620,000, an Extraordinary General Meeting was held. Despite an impressive slide show presentation detailing the increase in revenue that the extra capacity would bring, after just two hours the project was abandoned. A vote of thanks was extended to Bill Ramsay and others who had given much of their time to the project over the previous three-and-a-half years and a statement was issued to the press. Bill Ramsay continued as Honorary Treasurer and chairman of the Ground Sub-committee and soon after, as President of the RFU, left Buckingham Palace in the company of his wife and daughter-in-law as Sir William Ramsay.

Chapter Nine

PERFECT PITCH

Irrespective of all else that goes on inside a sports stadium, there is no more important ingredient than the surface on which the sport is played. At Twickenham, especially at the start of the season, there is no finer sight to greet the eye of one who appreciates a decent bit of turf than the pitch. Lush and cultivated to perfection, it has become something of a benchmark. But to sustain such a surface requires a lot of expertise, money and, particularly at Rugby HQ, a dedication often above and beyond the call of duty. More importantly than elsewhere at most other grounds, it has been the pitch that has determined the development of Twickenham.

Charlie Hale is traditionally credited as the groundsman who first laid out the Twickenham pitch. But in the RFU archive there is a faded photograph of one George A Street and family. So the postscript on the back of this photograph goes, George Street was a Surrey-born cricket ground manager who was invited by the RFU to lay out the first pitch at Twickenham. Beyond that brief reference, the name George Street is consigned to the compost heap of pitch history.

The only other confirmed sightings of early groundsman activity are two photographs showing a man remarkably similar in dress and appearance to George Street, but ascribed to Charlie Hale. These were taken during or after 1908 as the groundsman's cottage, newly built that year, features in the background alongside the new fencing lining Oak Lane (now Rugby Road). The character tending the fledgling pitch in 1908 looks to be more in his fifties than his twenties. At this time George Street would have been 53 years old and Charlie Hale, who retired in 1946, would have been about 27.

What is known for sure is that one of Charles Crane's first actions as newly appointed President of the Rugby Football Union (1907-8) was to arrange with the builders of the Metropolitan Railway for a dump of excavated soil at Twickenham to raise the seven-acre pitch as a defence against flooding and, after 1908, it was predominantly Charlie Hale and his sons who kept the grass long for half a century as the best means of managing Billy Williams's hugely disadvantaged discovery.

If it is possible to suggest a personal confrontation between man and turf, then that event arrived on St Valentine's Day 1964, when Twickenham's problematical playing surface was confronted by the arrival of a man with a particular affinity with grass and mud. Complete with a hearty dose of good old-fashioned, no-nonsense, Yorkshire grit, Harold Clark was a man who said what he saw, and what he saw at Twickenham left him much to say.

'What a tip the whole place was', his highly entertaining memoirs begin. An old urinal under the South Terrace was the ground staff mess. On the floor were the ground staff fast asleep with their coats laid over them. Custom and practice dictated that they helped themselves to beer when it was on the premises prior to a match, a tradition they continued with a passion. Whatever couldn't be drunk at the time was squirreled away in ovens, Wellington boots and behind girders. And some spectators were little better. The West Stand bar was about twenty metres long. When there were problems with serving a round of perhaps 30 pints, customers tired of waiting would climb over the bar to help themselves.

Overall, the bars at Twickenham were in a pitiful state, with no washing facilities for staff and those for washing glasses 'primitive' at best. Under the counters and throughout the stadium were wooden square bowls made of teak with lead linings. Water had to be kept in them to stop them drying out and cracking during the summer months. The water would then become stagnant and smelly. Clark immediately had these removed and replaced with modern stainless steel units. Then there were 156 public toilets complete with rusting and dilapidated cast iron cisterns, all of which took months to renew with modern plastic units.

Another huge challenge was the staff, comprising mainly casual labourers who swept the stands after matches and painted them in the summer months. Some were picked up at a local pub for the promise of free beer, others were sent along to 'find jobs' by Messrs Humphreys Ltd. Neither approach impressed the new clerk of works who informed Humphreys that men would turn up as and when they were requested, which resulted in Clark being reported to the RFU Ground Committee for 'being too keen'.

Effectively concluding the special relationship that had existed between Messrs Humphreys and the Rugby Football Union for almost 50 years, Harold Clark thereafter assembled a proper team with staff hired on recognised trades rates and conditions of service. Not that all members of the RFU approved of the 'modern ways' Clark had brought with him, but without question here was the right man to drag the ground kicking and screaming out of the Victorian age.

While the stadium generally was 'quite a dump', the pitch was a disaster. Ankle deep in mud, the battered turf had to cope with as many as eighteen Harlequins matches even before the first international was played. It was rolled every week to 'iron it out', but all that did was to compact the soil and prevent any penetration of surface water. In the summer, the pitch looked fine as the moisture was staying at the surface (along with the fertilizers) but in the winter, with so many games being played on it and the rainwater unable to drain away, the ground became a sea of mud.

As well as its location, there was the design of a stadium where the pitch and tall stands have to compete for natural ventilation and sunlight. Turf in shadow will not grow as vigorously as that enjoying good light. But the most significant feature of any pitch is what lies underneath it, in the sub-structure and drainage. Regular maintenance to the Twickenham pitch was little more than a forking over before a match, with the occasional application of fertilizer and a dressing of sand applied by means of a spiked roller. The most common cause of postponed matches is waterlogging or the pitch being frozen hard. Covering the surface with straw was a favourite remedy to prevent the latter. Sadly, nothing is recorded about the effect or otherwise of the magnificently whacky 'Jetaire Steam Heater' featured in a photograph, which blew hot air under a covering of tarpaulins to defrost the pitch.

The science of ground-keeping technology began in 1929 when the Sports Turf Research Institute was set up as the main centre of research to advise on the matter of pitch management. Men from the Ministry of Agriculture and Fisheries came to Twickenham in 1945 to examine the pitch, as did others from the Board of Green Keeping Research. Then in the spring of 1952, a new spiking machine was assessed and holes were bored to try and ascertain the condition of the original herringbone drainage system.

No other ground, including Wembley, was used as much as Twickenham with on average 30 matches played a year. As well as the eighteen Harlequins games and the internationals, there was the Varsity Match, the Middlesex Sevens, three Inter-Services matches, the schools internationals, the club knock-out final and the final trial. The pitch also had to cope with England squad training sessions and regular invasions by spectators.

In the opinion of the ground committee, the pitch was too overplayed to keep it in proper condition for international matches. Any of the Harlequins' matches could have been cancelled if deemed not beneficial to the pitch prior to an international, but none were. By February 1953, the condition of the pitch had deteriorated to such an extent that a proper drainage scheme was by now essential. W H Bowles, the head groundsman at Eton College and Chairman of the National Association of Groundsmen, was brought in to assess the situation.

Bowles confirmed the worst and recommended a pipe be taken into the perimeter drain around the playing field, six new draining sumps and deep spiking. Seven years later, three independent experts made as many separate inspections. One opinion expressed the view that the drainage remained good and the ground was improving. Others suggested a programme of seeding, spring fertilization, the purchase of more spiking equipment and a lighter tractor.

By the time Harold Clark arrived, thousands of pounds and as many hours had been expended on the pursuit of a problem that defied a solution, but which to him was obvious. The original drainage system had failed completely. As the top surface became so compacted, so the drains collapsed, creating stubborn waterlogged areas. Clark immediately stopped the process of rolling and planned a series of slits to be filled with coarse sand to help drain the surplus water. But so compacted was the ground that the spades were unable to go deep enough and all that happened was that the water stood in the slits. When the drains were opened where they were known to be, they were found to be some three feet deep. With no backfill, and with only black smelly clay and compacted soil to the surface, there was no option but to open up the whole playing area and properly drain it.

Having expressed his 'general dissatisfaction' in a stiff letter to the Sports Turf Research Institute, Harold Clark ploughed up the entire pitch using specialized equipment made by local engineers. Tons of sand was fed into slits over the full length of the playing area and by the time the French were challenging Welsh supremacy, the home of England Rugby could boast the best-drained pitch in the world, even if its inherent quality was still lacking, like the performance of the home team.

Whereas the Union had difficulty in reducing the number of games played, it did manage to refuse a number of financially lucrative opportunities. Despite revenue in the region of £40,000, American Football was dismissed, as was Lord Wakefield's suggestion of a motorcycle speedway, and bandsmen from the neighbouring Royal School of Military Music at Kneller Hall were denied use of the ground to put on their annual marching band display. Eventually, due to the unevenness of the pitch caused by its overuse, the decision was taken to reduce the numbers of games before 1st October each season.

Matches were restricted to the full set of Harlequins games in September, Oxford v Cambridge, a game against a major touring side, the England trials, two home internationals, the John Player Cup and the Middlesex Sevens. The Borough Sports Day, which had been held at Twickenham since 1929, was also retained. But in consolidating a policy with regard to the number of fixtures played, the RFU could not lose sight of Twickenham as 'Rugby's Mecca'.

It was the aspiration of every player to play there, whether representing country, division, county, club, service or university. Although it was recognised that such matches had evolved through national requirements, tradition and primacy in rugby-playing terms, the plea went out that the playing area was 'held most sacred'. Pitch condition for international matches was a source of pride and the protection of the playing surface the highest priority.

The Ground Committee set out a structured 'Twickenham season' with matches set at the most optimum time to preserve the pitch condition for internationals alone. Four sets of criteria determined which fixtures could continue. Top priority was England internationals, including World Cup, Five Nations and Touring Teams. Next came international England B, England Students, England Under 21s and England Schools. Third were the crowd-pulling games (of about 10,000 spectators) already on the calendar such as the Sevens, Cup and County Final, Oxford v Cambridge and Army v Navy.

Lastly came the traditional but poorly attended

matches (in hundreds), which included the Colts County Final, Harlequins games, RAF v RN and Army, England trials, Divisional v Touring and Junior Clubs Knock-out Final, and it was here that the greatest savings could be made in time, effort and wear and tear on the pitch. Despite these fixtures being important institutions in the development and promotion of the game, they were identified in the new language of the age as 'financial loss leaders'.

Apart from the costs of staff and ancillary services opening and manning the ground, it was argued that there was also the quality of the total experience set against a cavernous, hollow and poorly attended backdrop that did not add to inspiration or generally good rugby. Also, because of the cost of opening the ground compared with the rent paid for their matches, Harlequins were asked to find alternative venues for their games and did so in the 1960s.

Come the 1990s and the ground's lifelong tenants had already reduced their fixtures to three matches annually and were required to submit fixture details three years in advance for planning purposes. Conscious of their 'unique arrangement' over the lifetime of the stadium, Harlequins were prepared to give way to early season matches, but at the same time were looking to the end of their special relationship.

The Watchtower Bible and Tract Society (Jehovah's Witnesses) summer fixture was likewise under threat. The convention first hired the ground in 1954. The £3,000 paid for the five-day event was a welcome contribution during the non-playing season and in reality did little damage to the pitch with the judicial placing of its jumbo-sized baptismal immersion tank. But by the 1990s, it was felt that the convention was bringing about 'a fundamental change' caused by the 'antipathy amongst local residents' over fears of increased numbers. What this actually meant was that as the ground's capacity increased, so too did pressures on the RFU, which made the arrangement no longer practicable. That is until the RFU felt it 'could not afford to refuse' the £100,000 offered.

Pitch invasion continued to be 'disappointing without being disastrous' and likewise its share of exhibitionists and political protests over the years. The so-called South Africa 'demo-tour' of 1969-70 took place against the backdrop of a world community tightening the sanctions first imposed on South Africa in 1967 against the apartheid regime. The Rugby Football Union continued to support the South Africa tour to 'maintain its long-standing friendship'. South Africa, it argued, already enjoyed a multi-racial mix in its rugby football, trials and coaching, and the best way to work towards multi-racial sport was from within and not by withdrawing.

When streaking became fashionable in the '70s, a quick-thinking PC on duty for the England v France game in 1974 made famous use of his headgear. Two years later, another young man streaked in front of a 60,000 crowd during the Middlesex Sevens and was fined £20 by Richmond magistrates for 'insulting behaviour'. On 2nd January 1982, the day after Harold Clark handed over the reigns to his son, John, England were playing Australia. The new Clerk of Works was in the process of offering Bill Beaumont a piece of orange when Erica Roe streaked by. 'Blimey!' he thought, 'This isn't a bad job', just as another girl streaked by followed up by a gorilla.

The Diamond Vision Screens coming on line at this time showed player profiles, highlights of each team, great moments of past matches and the background to Twickenham. They also added to the problem of pitch invasion with hordes of spectators crowding onto an already pulped pitch to watch the post-match entertainment. The screens had been installed the previous year on completion of the South Stand. With its new bars and banqueting suite came the executive box and a screen was added in the north-east corner of the ground. Keen not to disenfranchise lesser mortals at the north end, another screen was provided at the south-west corner in time for the Calcutta Cup in March 1983.

Protecting Twickenham's problematic pitch was the job of the staunch core of yellow-coated stewards trained to display 'deference rather than confrontation'. Thus, the presence of 'girls' (*sic*) in the ranks was deemed acceptable and the idea of a rope cordon stretched between stewards was abandoned lest it upset the 'traditional very special relationship' between them and the spectators. Instead, reminder notes were enclosed with tickets, backed up by statements in programmes reiterated over the wonky public address system. In an ongoing attempt to educate the crowd to keep off the pitch, serious thought was given to the publishing of a mock-up photograph in match programmes showing what the pitch would look like surrounded by high wire fencing. It was even suggested that small children sat adjacent to the ground 'disciplined by their masters' to act as a human shield against potential pitch invasion.

Floodlighting is something that we take for granted these days. Incredibly, matches played at Twickenham continued to be governed by the setting of the sun either side of Christmas right up until 1995. Whereas some of the humblest grounds across the UK had long since enjoyed being able to maintain regular kick-off times, the matter first came up for discussion at Twickenham in February 1958. Five years later, a £4,000 portable kit, which could also be hired out to other grounds, was considered but the adventure was abandoned in favour a policy of no evening games or events brought about by floodlights, which would result in extra wear and tear on the pitch.

Richmond Rugby Football Club is often credited with hosting the first-ever experimental floodlit sporting event in 1878. But on 14th October 1874, 20,000 spectators packed Bramall Lane for a 7.30 pm kick-off to watch two Sheffield teams play a game of football illuminated by a 'soft blue light' given out by electric reflector lights mounted on four 30-foot wooden towers at each corner of the pitch. On 26th February 1889, the forerunners of Manchester United and Manchester City played an evening match to a far superior light created by high-pressure inflammable oil pumped to a burner that created a flare. Unfortunately this system not only burned a great deal of oil, but was also something of a fire risk. In 1892, Celtic experimented with a string of lamps tied to ropes hung 50 feet above the pitch, but the ball kept hitting the lamps. Another idea, which enjoyed limited success, was a spotlight used to follow a whitewashed ball.

Not that the RFU was necessarily alone in lagging behind the rest of the world, at least in the early days. The Football Association had placed a complete ban on any member clubs taking part in a floodlit match, including those at Wembley, which did not boast floodlighting until 1955. Portman Road was lit in 1959 at a cost of £15,000 and even non-league Leamington could boast floodlighting by 1964, having acquired Manchester City's old system. In 1972 Spurs upgraded its White Hart Lane system for the third time at a cost of £26,000. Its original system consisted of four poles at each corner of the pitch.

Twenty years later, and with the fate of Wembley hanging in the balance, came a golden opportunity to see Twickenham hosting national Football League matches, World Cup football, boxing, concerts and festivals. Together with recommendations of the Taylor Report post-Hillsborough highlighting an increased probability of delays to kick-off instigated by the police, the Union could delay the matter no longer. In looking for an immediate return on the estimated £1.05 million cost to floodlight the stadium, the Union's long-standing pitch protection policy was changed. England playing South Africa on 18th November 1995 was the first game to be played under floodlighting at Twickenham as the last major football ground in Britain to boast the facility.

In September 2002 came the news that the Rugby Football Union planned to build a new South Stand at Twickenham, while it also wrestled with the thorny matter of its grass. By this time plenty of alternative solutions were available to obviate the potentially lethal effects on a playing surface enclosed on all sides by high stands. The Sapporo Dome in Japan was hailed as one of the wonders of the sporting and architectural world with its giant Teflon-coated roof allowing sunlight in to kiss the spectacular 8,300 tonne pitch floated into the stadium on jets of air. The equally spectacular Stade de France in Paris allowed for the lower tier of seats to roll back, revealing an athletics track.

Another, less technologically daunting remedy is to regularly re-lay the playing surface. Such a procedure has been successfully carried out at Old Trafford since its hallowed turf was enclosed. The RFU's recruiting the necessary experience in the form of Manchester United's head groundsman therefore made eminent sense. An eight-metre strip of specially prepared synthetic grass made its debut at Twickenham on 9th November 2002 when England beat the All Blacks. Laid as a warm-up surface, it ran the length of the pitch in front of the West Stand. More a carpet of long-tufted fibres with a sand and rubber infill, it offered a surface claimed to closely resemble actual pitch conditions.

Although it was more of a promotion for use by clubs and schools for training, the impressive quality and durability of the surface, and its ability to fine-tune the synthetic grass close to actual playing conditions put a shiver down the spine of many a groundsman.

It was this very subject that one Twickenham guide was discussing with a man from Dingle who was in his 88th year and had left school at twelve to pursue a long career as a gardener. The two men talked about the problems of getting grass to grow in the Millennium Stadium in Cardiff. New technology meant that grass grown on pallets could be delivered and then grown inside the stadium where the roots would be stimulated by blowing warm air underneath. The Twickenham guide asked the man from Dingle for any clues as to why the new technology wasn't working. 'Sure,' replied the man, 'I left school at twelve and I know nothin'. But I do know that grass won't grow where the f***in' rain don't fall and where the f***in' sun don't shine.'

Chapter Ten

THE SPORTS GROUNDS ACT

With the fall of the original South Stand scheme, spare capital to hand was spent completing the Union's Whitton Road property portfolio and some general remedial work to the stadium. The old wooden ring seats in the North Stand were replaced with plastic benches on galvanized steel supports to provide for an additional 1,600 seats in readiness for the full programme of RFU centenary celebrations in 1971. But as the Rugby Football Union celebrated, so it was forced to look ahead. The days of running repairs and piecemeal opportunism were fast coming to an end. The value of sport and its attendant kudos among nations eager to host the great events was being reflected in the architecture and facilities of the venues.

In Britain after 1974, all stadia were required to obtain a licence in order to comply with a new Safety of Sports Grounds Act. The Greater London Council was the authority responsible for overseeing this work at all of the capital's grounds. At Twickenham it was agreed that Harold Clark would be given virtually free reign to meet the new regulations without having to go through the plethora of RFU committees. In so doing he produced twelve scale drawings, complete with every measurement and detail of lighting, gates, seating and staircases, etc.

Long before the horror of Hillsborough made it mandatory, the RFU was considering making Twickenham an all-seater stadium as the most effective means of controlling crowds of 72,000. A start was made in the East Stand by taking out the ring seating and terracing, replacing it with aluminium seating as a more permanent and maintenance-free alternative to wood and cast iron. Additional seating was found at the north terrace by moving the fencing back, but any benefits accruing was offset by the ongoing problems plaguing its counterpart at the south end of the stadium. Many attempts were made to keep the rain and frost out of its ageing joints, but the area below continued to be troubled by damp, with constant maintenance required to keep it not only safe but also healthy.

As part of the requirements under the Act, the capacity of the South Terrace was reduced to 15,000. The area was fast becoming uneconomic as that number would probably need pruning even more. The steelwork, subject to such severe encrustation and contraction of the concrete cladding, had deteriorated to such an extent that any further remedial work would be self-defeating. Patchwork repairs without proper waterproofing could not protect it from progressive corrosion. Already the South Terrace was fast reaching its margins of safety. The Ground Committee was reminded of the Kennedy and Donkin Report of 1956 that gave the life of the South Terrace as a maximum 25 years and that limit was fast approaching.

No detailed plans, drawings or specifications of its construction existed to guide the consultants in a rational course of action, which left the Union with no other financially viable option but to rebuild. The cost of this was estimated at around £125,000. Added to this, other parts of the stadium had also been identified as requiring even more urgent attention. Consulting engineers Jan Bobrowski and Partners established that the steelwork to the North, East and West Stands was in good, serviceable condition and well maintained, but there was evidence of extensive cracking to the concrete reinforcing the steel bars to the lower areas due to water penetration.

The Lower East Stand especially was suffering from extensive cracking to the first ten rows, which would persist irrespective of the thickness of any remedial concrete cladding. The entire structure had generally widened due to corroded reinforcements, with possible serious consequences under full load conditions. Despite this, the entire skin of corrugated iron cladding was replaced for the Union's centenary year. For ease of construction and to enable a reduced time span, a reconstruction of the affected areas using pre-tensioned units of the finest quality concrete was estimated in the region of £50,000. When translated to 1978 cost terms, this hovered between £93,000 and £165,000. With the all-important safety certificate allowing for fewer than 70,000 spectators, such a severe impact on Twickenham's long-term financial viability turned attention again to the idea of moving to pastures new.

Deeming it 'unlikely' that an alternative site would be found and accepting the expectation that rugby would be played at Twickenham for at least the next 25 years, the RFU looked to the concept of a commercial property developer underwriting a South Stand and of sharing the ground with other sports and events to ensure a satisfactory annual income. Almost £300,000 was spent on fulfilling the requirements of the Safety Act, largely committed to the Lower East

Stand and converting standing areas to seats. Even though grant aid was available to underwrite some of the costs, only £85,000 was received. Yet £17,000 was found from Union coffers to acquire number 212 Whitton Road and £230,000 for the building of a new suite of offices.

Chapter Eleven

THE SOUTH STAND

The years between 1969 and 1979 were not happy ones for the English game. Apart from a five-way tie in 1973, a championship for Ireland the following year and France winning the Grand Slam in 1977, these were the glory days for Wales, who won three Grand Slams, four other championships and twice shared the booty. Throughout this decade, Wales and France were in one league, Ireland and Scotland in another while England skulked somewhere in the shadows. But soon there would be not so much a wind of change, more a hurricane that would revolutionise the game and the lives of those who played it and those who administered it.

Replacing the South Terrace was optimistically estimated at £1,040,000, which was considered excessive. Consultants Bobrowski and Partners were asked to produce a radical downsizing of the proposed new stand to exclude the roof, lifts, entertainment boxes and banqueting facilities; retaining only the standing areas or double-tiered seating levels. By December 1978, the costs had reached £2 million, which forced the RFU to look for an even more economical scheme, ideally a basic structure that allowed for future development without incurring later planning consent.

The existing South Terrace consisted of 85 concrete steps on exposed steel framing, with the width varying depending on the location over an area of 31,000 square metres. The dimensions in no way met the requirements of the Safety Act. The number of exits was inadequate and there was no roof coverage. The facilities beneath the massive concrete raft included a public first aid room, a stewards' restaurant, a kitchen and food preparation room, public toilets, the cushion store, programme control, a ground staff room, a large bar, a tobacco and confectionery kiosk, various storage facilities and two public telephones; all of which were only part covered and enclosed by face brickwork.

Even with all the major remedial work done to bring the structure up to standard, the reduction in the numbers of spectators would lead to a considerable loss of income, which over time would threaten the entire Twickenham operation. Also, to conform to existing building regulations and the requirements of the Safety Act, the stadium would have to cut into the gardens of the houses at the rear of the South Terrace, which was unacceptable to the planning authority. There was little choice in the matter. If the South Terrace was not rebuilt then the licensing authority would require the existing structure to be demolished. Biting the bullet, an outline planning application was submitted to local and GLC planning offices on 2nd March 1979 in preparation for meetings before their summer recess.

The brochure prepared by the architects showed a basic plan of the proposed new South Stand, which resulted in compliance in principle. But with the costs now raised to £2.4 million, a Special General Meeting was called for 30th March where the case was made for a stand comprising two tiers providing accommodation for 5,700 standing and 5,500 seated and with the existing ring seating of 1,048 retained. Other facilities would be provided depending on demand. At an estimated cost of £2,070,000, reckoned to increase by another £400,000 per year in building costs and inflation – not to mention the volatility of oil prices upsetting the market – the RFU could not afford to delay.

Building the South Stand created a fundamental change in the attitude of the RFU hierarchy. The bank was prepared to lend upwards of £3 million, but on terms so unfavourable that the Union was forced to look elsewhere. The firm of Richard Costain Ltd made various (undisclosed) approaches to the local authorities as well as some 'unofficial enquiries' to the GLC for a financially self-supporting scheme to develop Twickenham. But it was the rival firm of Wates Ltd who first presented the scenario for a pedestrian precinct and entrance stretching the length of Whitton Road. Funding it was a Woolco supermarket in the west car park for use by customers on all but major RFU occasions. But this was considered by the local authority to be 'quite out of keeping with the general character of the ground'.

Another option was put forward by the ASDA supermarket chain for a 60,000 square foot retail development in the north car park, which was also met with a huge wave of indifference by the planning authorities. Crystal Palace FC had encountered the same difficulties with a similar scheme, so directors of the club were asked how they did it. But Palace officials were not prepared 'to divulge their method and means' without payment. Instead, they set up a company to supply the necessary expertise for the RFU to obtain planning approval.

With an expected annual rent in the region of £100,000 and with ASDA willing to cover all the costs arising, the Union was prepared to go to appeal if the planning application was denied. Both Richmond and Hounslow boroughs were vehemently opposed to the scheme on the grounds that the area around the stadium was zoned primarily for residential purposes. As well as poor road access, there was another supermarket being developed in Twickenham town centre. That this invalidated the building of another in the district demonstrates just how much market forces have changed in 30 years.

After it was eventually decided not to proceed in this direction, a scheme was put forward by a firm of international architects to include 100 residential flats. This was rejected for being 'too much out of proportion with the remainder of the stands'. Thoughts then turned to a hotel being incorporated into a new South Stand complex. This did find favour with the planning authorities, but sadly attracted no interest from the various brewery groups and hotel chains approached. Enquiries made to brand names with a view to their sponsoring the new stand, similar to the Warner Stand at Lord's, proved similarly fruitless. Despite a growing preparedness to think outside of its box, the RFU was still fighting shy of embracing full-on commercialism such as corporate hospitality, so it returned to the tried and trusted method of debentures to raise the cash.

So clear a course of action was corporate hospitality to everyone else outside of Rugby HQ, that consulting architects, the Lobb Partnership, incorporated two demonstration boxes for their own use at no cost to the RFU as a means of demonstrating their viability and profitability. Meanwhile, marketing gurus Bagnal Harvey did manage to get the Union to agree to a 'low-key start' on the corporate hospitality ladder in the form of four tents pitched on the 'front lawn' (the grassed area at the junction of Whitton and

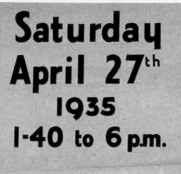

Saturday April 27th 1935
1·40 to 6 p.m.

7 A-SIDE FINALS
at
TWICKENHAM

Admission 1/- Rover Tickets & Ring Seats 2/6
Special Reserved Tickets (Centre Blocks West Stand) 5/-
(Numbers Strictly Limited)

THE PROCEEDS WILL BE GIVEN TO THE MIDDLESEX HOSPITAL CANCER FUND

TICKETS FROM :—Messrs. Alfred Hays Ltd., 26 Old Bond Street, W.I. (Regent 4040) ; 74 Cornhill, E.C. (Avenue 1466) ; 62 Strand, W.C. (Temple Bar 3032.) The Assistant Secretary : Middlesex Hospital, W.I. The Secretary, Rugby Union, Twickenham, or any member of the Middlesex County R.F.U.

Twickenham at war. Sandbags in the North Stand (above) and coal in the West Car Park (below). (RFU)

Ladies occupy the Committee Members' tea room (above) and the West Stand restaurant becomes a First Aid Post. (RFU)

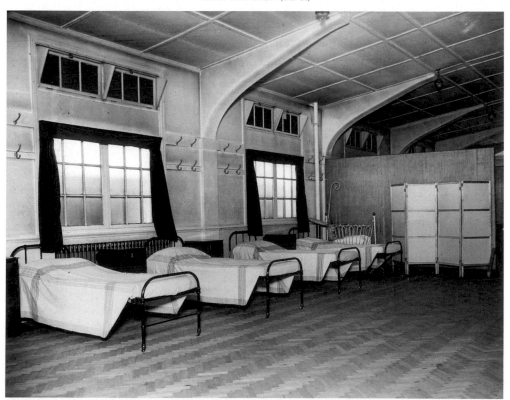

Protecting the pitch with straw and hot air. (RFU)

Twickenham in the '60s by local artist Philip Poyser. (Brian Pearce)

"EVERLASTING GOOD NEWS" Assembly of
JEHOVAH'S WITNESSES, Twickenham, July 14-21

Everlasting Good News for the RFU's coffers with Twickenham the focus for Jehovah's Witnesses.

Twickenham in the '80s. A new South Stand and marketing makes an appearance. (RFU)

The demolition of Leitch's North Stand heralds a new '90s era. (author)

The new North Stand, the longest cantilever roof in Britain, and the museum adding to the 'Twickenham Experience'. (RFU

(Mike Cherry)

1994. The old West Stand makes way for the new. Floodlights make their debut at the ground a year later. (RFU)

Issue No.11 January 2000

RUGBY POST

RUGBY FOOTBALL UNION

The RFU Community Newsletter

International Athletics and Twickenham Stadium

Twickenham Stadium has been identified as a possible venue to stage the World Athletics Championships in 2005 and for a possible future bid to host the 2012 Olympic Games.

With Wembley no longer a consideration to host athletics, the Twickenham option has been discussed by the RFU, the Government, the British Olympic Association and UK Athletics.

A feasibility study carried out by the RFU has confirmed that Twickenham Stadium could host athletics, subject to planning consent, a redevelopment of the South Stand and the necessary investments required to improve the existing road and rail links.

The way forward is likely to depend on UK Athletics' decision whether to bid to stage the 2005 world championships. A decision is expected at the end of January. If the RFU is part of that bid, then discussions will begin with all the relevant parties including the London Boroughs of Richmond upon Thames and Hounslow, the police, transport authorities, local MPs and residents.

Francis Baron, the RFU's Chief Executive, said: "When the Government approaches you to do something like this for British sport you feel you want to help. However, we will have to consider carefully whether this makes good business sense. There are a number of important issues involved, most notably our local community and the transport infrastructure needed to enable this scale of event."

INSIDE THIS ISSUE	Match Day Controlled Parking Zones	Local Residents' Ticket Ballot	A Brief History of Twickenham Stadium

FREE TICKETS FOR DAILY MAIL SCHOOLS DAY AT TWICKENHAM - *SEE INSIDE*

A New Millennium and new plans for the Cathedral of Rugby. (RFU)

Images of Twickenham by local artist Jill Storey. (Jill Storey)

RUGBY FOOTBALL UNION COMMUNITY MAGAZINE   ISSUE 21 – WINTER 2003

RFU

RUGBY POST

IN THIS ISSUE

PROPOSED NEW SOUTH STAND FOR TWICKENHAM

MUSIC DAY RAISES £10,000 FOR LOCAL CHARITIES

THE MOBILE YOUTH CAFE TAKES TO THE ROAD

RICHMOND UPON THAMES SCHOOLS' SPORTS DAY

HOMELINK –A LOCAL CHARITY WORTH SUPPORTING

SATISFACTION AS STONES COME HOME

Twickenham finally got what it wanted when the world's greatest rock and roll band, The Rolling Stones, played two sold out concerts at the home of English rugby.

One hundred thousand attended both concerts including around 10,000 local people from Richmond upon Thames and Hounslow and almost 10,000 visitors from abroad.

Operationally, both concerts went extremely well and the RFU is grateful for the support of Richmond and Hounslow Council officers and members,

South West Trains, London United Buses, the police, emergency services, as well as local residents who contributed to the organization of the concerts through the RFU's Concert Day Committee and Neighbours' Liaison Group.

RFU Community Relations Officer, Fraser Cullen said, "From the feedback received, many of the borough's residents thoroughly enjoyed being part of these historic events for Twickenham and seeing the greatest rock and roll band in the world. We hope that the local residents who couldn't get tickets and either stood around the stadium or partied in their gardens will be able to attend future concerts."

PROMOTING TWICKENHAM AROUND THE WORLD

The concert on Sunday 24th August was filmed and will be released as one of a four DVD set titled 'Four Flicks' and released on November 10th. The world wide sales will ensure that Twickenham is promoted around the globe.

ENGLAND MATCHES TICKET BALLOT
ENGLAND V IRELAND, ENGLAND V WALES - P8

From cabbages to concerts and news of a new South Stand. (RFU)

Sunday 10th July 2005 'Operation Blowdown' for the South Stand.(Author)

A century on from William Cail's vision and Twickenham comes full circle. (British Library/Author)

Rugby Roads). England playing host to Wales on 16th February 1980 was chosen as the most suitable date.

Despite the violence that marred the game, the Union earned more than £2,500, which effectively opened the door for this and other untapped streams of fresh revenue, long enjoyed at other major and minor grounds. Twickenham's famous weathervane and the RFU Rose were registered in readiness for the dawn of something called merchandising, which was by this time not only desirable but increasingly essential. The debentures scheme was struggling to meet costs of the South Stand close to £4 million. With less than a third of that amount accrued, the scheme was saved by a combination of a bank overdraft to be repaid in three years, delayed payments to the contractors and a £500,000 grant from the Sports Council.

Demolition of the old South Terrace began on 6th May 1980 with Alf Wright bemoaning the loss of the great concrete raft. 'They brought in cranes with great iron balls on the end of chains to knock the place down,' he recalled. 'When they dropped the iron balls on the concrete, they just bounced. It took them over a fortnight to knock it down. Unsafe indeed!' Certainly as the demolition progressed, so the bad state of decay was confirmed.

After seeing a model of the proposed stand, a similarly unconvinced Harold Clark tried to persuade the Ground Committee not to build it. It was not, after all, a football stand, but one designed for racing. The same stand had been built at Goodwood Racecourse. It was only when the work was completed that the committee agreed with Clark that it should never have been built. Others felt that it represented the best value for money and in design the most sympathetic to the temperamental playing area.

Boasting room for more than 5,500 spectators seated in two tiers and nineteen rows, and 6,200 spectators on 32 rows of standing terrace, the bare bones of the new South Stand were completed in time for the England v Scotland match on 21st February 1981. Two years and around £1.6 million later, the Rose Room banqueting suite, a museum and shop opened for the first home international (15th January 1983). A growing commercial confidence expressed itself in an agreement with the marketing firm of West Nally, which allowed them the sole rights from the twelve executive boxes. At an estimated basic £370,000 return with a turnover of some £600,000, it was decided that the £370,000 should be paid to the Union irrespective of bookings, which still left West Nally with a healthy share in the enterprise.

Come the 1980s and with ever increasing demands on the players, the RFU looked at the world outside their own rarefied atmosphere and began to question their amateur status. Sponsorship was by now acceptable. Indeed the Union had been scandalised for accepting money from a company of boot manufacturers. British rugby was in something of a twilight zone, caught between the amateur principle and the inevitable professional era. During the emergence of 'Corporate Twickenham', another important element of the marketing strategy seen as 'vital to progress' was the public face of the organisation.

The first RFU shop proved a huge success, selling branded RFU merchandise and souvenirs. Number 180 Whitton Road, now home to Alf Wright who had taken on the role of consultant historian/curator after retiring as assistant secretary, became the site of Twickenham's first museum and reference library. So attached had Alf become to the piles of paper and artefacts swelling the top floor of his abode that RFU officials had to pay a visit to 'relieve' him of material destined for the new museum in the West Stand. Sadly, they found little of interest and so the opening of the RFU Museum had to be delayed and the spare capacity was used as a VIP reception in conjunction with the highly successful Rose Room. In 1983 the Union created a proper, purpose-built museum and library facility in the South Stand.

Another element of this new public face of the RFU was the idea of guided stadium tours. However, the Union's commercial awareness was still very much in the development stage. Instead of employing acknowledged professional expertise, the views of Lord Montague and the Marquis of Bath were thought to be the best bet. Likewise it was believed that a joint venture with the Wimbledon Lawn Tennis Museum would somehow 'greatly increase visitors to Twickenham and the RFU Shop'. Fortunately, a representative of the West Nally Marketing group with experience at Wembley Stadium stepped in and suggested that the RFU needed to engage the services of a professional tour operator. Five 'dummy run' tours were proposed, starting with schools. Complete with a video presentation, the first official tour of the ground took place at 11 am on 20th November 1984.

Chapter Twelve

THE NORTH STAND

The new South Stand enjoyed all too briefly the role of catalyst leading the way to the 21st century. For no sooner did it appear than it became yesterday's dream. The demands of ground safety legislation had reduced the stadium's capacity to 62,000, a reduction of some 13,000 international match-day tickets, or one fifth of gate revenue. While the local authority matched government enthusiasm in looking to Twickenham to host the 1991 World Cup, the business of receiving and accommodating an estimated 70,000 increased capacity posed real problems.

Also, together with France, Scotland, Wales and Ireland, who for the most part had formed the 20th century's only universally acknowledged championship in the form of the Five Nations, there was no room for complacency in England Rugby and its governing body. Better rugby was being played in the southern hemisphere by New Zealand, Australia and South Africa, which together created a Rugby World Cup in 1987. As well as the game requiring a fundamental shift in the sporting calendar, it needed to extend itself beyond its Five Nations clique.

To this end, the RFU looked much further ahead to the vision of a fully enclosed stadium with a potential capacity of 120,000 spectators. By now with little option but to press on with a replacement North Stand, architects Husband and Co were appointed in June 1988, thus forging a partnership in the new

'Masterplan for Twickenham'. One suggestion was for 3,500 extra seats divided among the four corners of the stadium, giving a total capacity of 65,000. But the only real option was to demolish Archibald Leitch's quietly understated North Stand and replace it with one similar in scale to the new South Stand.

With the ringside seats likewise left in place and based on the assumption that the lower tier remained all standing, this would provide accommodation for an additional 4,000 spectators. With supplementary car parking at Twickenham now a planning requirement, added to which were the restrictions imposed by the allotments to the rear of the North Stand, this meant that the height of a new stand was a prime design consideration.

The Union boasted an architect and a quantity surveyor in its ranks, and, given that the organisation had gone through an architect-led approach with regard to the building of the South Stand, it was felt that the way forward was that of an informed client. Unfortunately, the combination of car parking and allotments was to prove near-lethal and would have perhaps been better left to the professionals to resolve.

This long-running saga began when the remaining six-and-a-half acres of the former Erncroft Estate became surplus to local authority requirements and for the third time in its history was on offer to the RFU. Its purchase would have in one clean sweep resolved the omnipresent problem of car parking and was all the more desirable as increasingly land to the north of the ground was being allocated to residential development. Despite encouragement from the council to purchase this prime piece of real estate, the RFU again found more urgent need of its capital, and worse, decided that the allotment land sandwiched between the west car park and the Duke of Northumberland's river represented by far the better option.

On hearing that the Ministry of Defence was thinking of closing the Royal Military School of Music at Kneller Hall, a plan was hatched for land associated with it to be 'exchanged' for the allotments. But such was the level of dissent against its closure that Kneller Hall was saved, leaving the RFU bogged down in the messy business of trying to acquire the allotments outright.

Whereas the six-and-a-half acres on offer from the council for £780,000 would have cut a mighty swathe through the perennial parking problem, the RFU set aside £1.1 million for the purchase of Rosebine Avenue, the long strip of open land half a mile from the ground immediately west of the Stoop Memorial Ground on the wrong side of the Chertsey Road. Added to this amount was an additional £250,000 for the preparation of new allotments on this land.

So eager was the Union to proceed that it agreed to pay £1.2 million for the land even before agreement was reached with the local authority and the Department of the Environment for the transfer to take place. Then there were the allotment holders themselves who were less than enthusiastic about the proposed resettlement package. As knowledge of plans to rebuild the North Stand came into the public domain, so a period of acrimony set in. Eventually, it was agreed to resite a minimum number of allotments north of their original position in the west car park area, leaving the RFU able to bring into use about half of its Rosebine investment as additional car parking.

The actual footprint of the proposed new structure

aside, a replica South Stand was immediately discounted due to its racetrack pedigree. In terms of stadium evolution, such architecture does not provide the required flexibility and level of options available. What was on the table for Twickenham was the first three-tier stand in the UK with the capacity to 'bolt on' new stands to its East and West ends at some future date. Cost being the key deciding factor, this type of construction allowed for the supporting framework, some sixty per cent of the structural content including the all-important seating, to be built first. Other requirements, such as lifts and bars, representing the remaining 40% of construction costs, could be added later.

Predictably, this ambition did not meet with unanimous approval. The very idea of accommodating spectators 100 feet above the pitch attracted criticism from those who felt that the rugby spectator would be too far removed from the action. In actual fact, the design envisaged the furthest vantage points only six metres further than corresponding seats in the South Stand and with sightlines superior to some of those in both the East and West Stands.

Whereas the Union had previously toyed with the idea of Twickenham becoming an all-seater stadium, it was now forced down this road as a requirement following the tragedy at Hillsborough in April 1989 when 96 soccer fans died. What had started out as a modest £168,000 investment aimed primarily at satisfying requirements under the Safety of Sports Grounds Act was now looking to blossom into an enterprise to the tune of £16 million.

Until the outcome of the inquiry into Hillsborough was known, the Union was taking a calculated risk in proceeding with any work on a new North Stand. This called for a close working relationship with the local authority Health and Safety team, which, despite a less than comfortable history, reaped dividends.

Fortunately, the main recommendations made by the inquiry were correctly anticipated. The timespan available was used wisely to reconfigure the build from a 20,000 mixed capacity to a 15,000 all-seater facility. Approval sought for the North Stand to be all-seating not only improved safety but also the prospect of satisfying planning permission. The assessment of the results in consultation with the Sports Turf Research Institute concluded that the proposed cantilever roof would have no adverse effect on the growth of the grass or its ability to dry out. But to ensure that adequate light made its way to the pitch, it was suggested that translucent panels were installed in the roof, not only to assist the groundsman, but also to reduce the intensity of the shadows and to improve the quality of television pictures.

When it came to the quotations received from the six construction firms vying for the contract, the RFU found itself extremely disappointed. Artificially high construction rates, created by the Docklands building boom in east London, ranged from Wimpey UK's £17.6 million to £16.4 million from the preferred contractor, Cementation Construction. After requesting a revisit of these tenders to see what savings could be made, the contract was passed over to Wimpey UK, which came in at £13.9 million (excluding the cost of seating in the lower stand). With the upper and middle tiers approved under the Safety of Sports Grounds Act and the lower tier awaiting revised plans, demolition of the old North Stand started two weeks before schedule on 20th May 1989.

The remaining cast iron and oak seats were sent to grace Harlequins' home ground at The Stoop, but another important element of the ground's history in the form of the groundsman's cottage slipped silently into the ether. Constructed before the pitch was prepared and a year prior to the first stand erected in 1909, this was Twickenham's first-ever built structure. It was home to the ground's first paid employee in the form of head groundsman and later the first Clerk of Works, Harold Clark. Unlike its listed namesake at Fulham's ground, the cottage at Twickenham was torn down to make way for a new workshop without a hint of sentiment based on history or heritage.

Likewise Archibald Leitch's North Stand, shrouded in its overcoat of painted corrugated iron. By July, the site where it once stood was peppered with 300 holes piled 30 metres deep, ready for the ground beams to take the first tier. A month later and rows of green plastic seats were being fitted at the rate of 1,000 per week. With work to the lifts and escalators in hand, a major extract of the Hillsborough Report was circulated together with a sense of unease at HQ that its author, Lord Justice Taylor, was to visit Twickenham to watch the Barbarians v New Zealand and the Varsity Match.

The lower stand was finished in time for his Lordship's first visit. The Safety Certificate was awarded on 17th November and the 6,143-seat section handed over to the RFU. With the pre-constructed pieces of the two upper tiers slotted into place, they opened a week later, maintaining a ground capacity in excess of 60,000 for the home international season the following January. The final Hillsborough Report recommended reduced standing at all football grounds by twenty per cent. With this already achieved in the new North Stand and with 3,071 tip-up seats to be installed at the South Stand the following season, Twickenham could already boast a fifty per cent reduction.

Despite a three-day steel strike and the insolvency of one contractor, the middle tier and 32 boxes were completed, and with two-thirds of the roof to follow, the Topping Out ceremony took place on 21st September 1990. Wide concourses to each tier provided for ease of entry and safe exit in the event of an emergency. Stairways wound around the main columns and lifts to the upper levels to access the enhanced spectator facilities.

Unlike a mere decade earlier, huge emphasis was now placed on corporate hospitality. There were 521 boxes with an exclusive debenture lounge, high quality bars, refreshment areas and toilet facilities long enjoyed by cash-rich Association Football counterparts. The longest cantilever roof in Britain not only provided weather protection and guaranteed sightlines, but truly usurped the South Stand as the benchmark for Twickenham's entry into the 21st century. A press clipping pasted into one of the many private scrapbooks donated to the RFU's Museum of Rugby, recalls Billy Williams 'who in 1908 let his cabbage patch become the first national sports ground of any rugby union'. A thoughtful tribute, but one doubtless irksome to the Unions of Wales, Scotland and Ireland who had established home grounds long before the idea had even occurred to the Rugby Football Union.

The new addition to Twickenham, standing tall and aloof, overwhelmed its southern counterpart in height, bulk and design and left the grand old dames of Twickenham's past with limited dates on their dance cards. In the Union's roll-out of its strategy, the stadium as it stood looked to a ten-year development plan from 1991 to 2001 with a number of key assumptions. The core objective was to raise capacity to 72,000 in time for the 1991 World Cup.

If the three-tier option was continued at the East and West Stands, then future capacity could be raised to 75,000. Reconfiguring the old stands would have been cheaper and easier but would have cut into capacity. Although both stands still had a life expectancy of 15 years, they were expensive to maintain and would prove increasingly so. Besides, they had no place in the RFU's vision of a 21st-century Twickenham. The stadium as it stood looked 'incongruous and demonstrably incomplete'. The decision was taken for the complete refurbishment of the largest dedicated rugby stadium in Europe.

Chapter Thirteen

THE EAST STAND

The core objective of the 'Strategy for Twickenham' was an effective administration structure required to take the Union into the 21st century. In common with so many other traditional organisations at this time, something called 'good management practice' would be introduced to make it easier for ideas and proposals to filter throughout the business and even make it to the full committee.

The game in England had grown in such size and complexity of its administration that as many changes were required off the pitch as planned on it and around it. Beyond the game, the Union's resolve was clear and succinct: 'to balance judiciously the requirements of the game with those projects which show immediate return on capital investment'.

Forming the central thrust of the strategy was a £27 million East Stand development and later a £32 million western counterpart. The South Stand was to remain for the foreseeable future. With the North Stand ready for containment into new East and West developments, Husband and Co undertook the application for the proposed new East Stand. The timing was excellent as inflation was down and the '90s building boom was over. Contractors were looking for work, which meant that construction costs could be driven down. The Union felt it 'should not delay in testing the water'.

The ground staff was congratulated on the

preservation of the pitch during the 1991 World Cup even though, and reminiscent of similar commentary 80 years earlier, it was felt that the grass was being kept too long. A balance had been struck to optimise the preservation of the pitch throughout the season, which took the form of a strict policy designed to keep the grass at no more than two inches in length, to be cut exactly to this length before each match day, weather permitting. England had lost out to Australia in the first Rugby World Cup in 1987, but had won the Grand Slam. The once mighty Wales had suffered their first whitewash in the Five Nations since the competition began shortly after Twickenham's virgin turf was first criticised.

With regard to the perennial issue of car parking, discussions had taken place with the Hounslow and Spelthorne Health Authority, and later with potential developers, over the derelict South Middlesex Hospital site to the north of Rugby Road. What was known as the Mogden Lane car park had been used to park an extra 350 cars and the Orchard Car Park due south used mostly for hospitality, but here again the RFU had shown little interest in going the extra mile and purchasing this land.

The RFU minuted its 'considerable regret' that planning approval had been won by Tesco to build a superstore and high density housing on the 30-acre site. Following an appeal by the RFU and the local authority to the Secretary of State, Tesco agreed to close the proposed store on match days at 11.00 am or two hours before kick-off for those matches attracting in excess of 30,000 spectators to a maximum of 10 days a year. Thus was created the only Tesco store in the country to close on a Saturday.

Despite making available to the Union an extra 680

spaces, the nightmare of attempting to park upwards of 9,000 cars meant looking at every park, school, college, council depot, bus garage and open space within a two-mile radius of the ground. A particular eye was cast on the Cardinal Vaughn playing fields north-west of the ground across the Duke's river. This was capable of accommodating 1,200 cars on match days, but would require the building of a footbridge to link the sites.

Although initially refused on grounds of safety and administration, a 99-year lease was eventually acquired by the RFU with an expensive proviso to build two soccer pitches, a Tarmac area with four tennis courts, two five-a-side football pitches, a new sports pavilion and a road to the car park area. Then in January 1992, the local authority expressed its 'total support' for the removal of the allotments at the north end of the ground, declaring 'the considerable benefits to be self-apparent'. Divided as it is between the London Boroughs of Richmond and Hounslow, the North Car Park was inspected by Hounslow Borough's valuation department to determine how the allotments intruded on RFU property and how many were actually used. The Union's need to buy all the allotment land owned by Richmond was accepted and allotment holders were offered generous financial incentives to vacate.

Although the RFU was 'appalled' by the decision to allow Tesco planning permission for a superstore and housing development, it did serve to stimulate progress at Twickenham. Building the proposed new 22,500 capacity East Stand before their arrival would thwart the likely objections from a fresh contingent of neighbours. Design-wise the new 25,000 capacity East Stand was a larger repetition of the North Stand, so all of its costs and contingencies could be accurately calculated to within 10 per cent. This offered a basic replacement stand estimated at around £18 million, plus fees.

On 15th January 1992, tenders were put out to Mowlem, Trafalgar House (formerly Cementation), Tarmac, Higgs and Hill, Wimpey, McAlpine and Fairclough. When the tenders were opened, the RFU was delighted by their attractively low costs. Mowlem South-East was the preferred contractor on account of its experience in building the North Stand. With the same military precision dictating the least disruption to the playing season, work began on removing the 17,000 seats in the East Stand on 11th May 1992. By the summer, with work progressing satisfactorily, the 'Strategy for Twickenham' was on course and under budget.

Encouraged by the success of the North Stand debenture scheme, more than £8.3 million was raised in the form of 1,000 business debentures, 10,000 individual debentures and 700 car park debentures. The cost of demolishing a stand far more formidable and a good one-third larger than the North Stand came in at about £4 million less. The first phase was completed by 7th November 1992 with 10,500 seats installed in the lower tier giving an overall ground capacity of 54,000. Harking back eight decades to when the ground first opened, the RFU minutes reflect the same resentment expressed by occupants of the press box who bemoaned the poor view and 'spartan conditions' they were expected to endure in the middle tier. Otherwise, it was to the RFU's credit that the emphasis remained on space for the committed rugby supporter and not the casual corporate hospitality guest.

But the lifeblood of sporting stadia worldwide was moving towards such revenue streams, which no organisation could afford to turn away. A compromise had to be found that would allow for corporate accommodation in any future development as being additional to capacity and not at the expense of it. It was therefore down to the architects, consultants and others to finance these additional elements in return for a guaranteed supply of corporate hospitality tickets.

One of these 'outsourced' elements was the Obolensky Restaurant, named after Alexander Obolensky, the Russian Prince who played right wing for England and who, in 1936, scored what is considered its greatest ever try. Having put a more conventional five points on the board, 'Obo' then wrong-footed the entire All Blacks team by running diagonally through the visitors to score a remarkable left-winger's try. The Wakefield Restaurant takes its name from William Wavell ('Wakers') Wakefield, who with his emphasis in the 1920s on a scientific system of back row defence formed the key to England's success in the period known as 'The Wakefield Era'. The winner of 31 caps and elected 42nd President of the RFU 1950-51, he was raised to the peerage as Baron Wakefield of Kendal in 1963.

On 29th October 1993, the dramatic 'Union' sculpture adorning the new stand's exterior was unveiled by the President of the Rugby Football Union, I D S Beer, in the presence of its creator, the entertainer, Tommy Steele, virtually completing the new stand on time and at a cost of £12.08 million. Twickenham was ready to host a total 68,000 capacity crowd for England v New Zealand on 7th November, giving a shortfall of only 4,800 seats over previous capacity.

The inaugural meeting of the museum working party, which took place six months later, looked to play a key role in the newly branded 'Twickenham Experience' with a £981,200 'live' content as opposed to a static display.

In confirming that the presence of this prestigious facility could only add to the financial benefits accrued from the RFU Shop and wide variety of catering facilities, the Union acquired 'The Harry Langton Collection', undoubtedly the most important collection of rugby memorabilia to become available. The RFU Museum of Rugby opened as one of the best interactive sports museums in the world in December 1995, at the heart of a stand boasting more accommodation than the entire capacity of any English rugby club.

Chapter Fourteen

THE WEST STAND

In the RFU's opinion, the catalyst for success at Twickenham thus far was 'undoubtedly the exceptional liaison' between it, the Husband Design Group, Mowlem and the local authority. With the low construction prices coming to an end, the decision was taken that there would be no better time to go for broke and rebuild the West Stand. Although it was a like-for-like construction, the cost would be double that of the East Stand due to a more complicated design. A further £9 million for a high-specification fitting-out process would make the new addition special.

Planning permission presented on 22nd March 1994 was met with only relatively minor objections, and work began immediately after the Middlesex Sevens final with the salvaging of artefacts before the less subtle stage of the process began.

Predictably, Alf Wright was unconvinced. He reckoned that knocking down the celebrated West Stand was nothing short of sacrilege. 'With every seat built onto a girder, it might have stood for a thousand years,' he lamented. Certainly, something went from Twickenham. Many a pundit opined that it was the height and the shape of the old stands that gave the ground its particular charm and character. Turning it into another oval, like Wembley, considered some, lost it its individuality. One contributor to a 1999 Rugby World Cup website bemoaned the 'strange lack of atmosphere' and longed for the days when 'fans stood side by side in the four old "cow-sheds" that perched along the edge of the pitch'. Quite what ground he was talking about is not clear.

Indeed the atmosphere may have suffered and the new Twickenham Look was by no stretch of the imagination pretty. The financial demands of its rebuilding was in keeping with the times where major building schemes and even domestic architecture called for a low-maintenance, inexpensive, simplistic finish of exposed concrete, breeze block and steel. But even the most ardent critic of the structure would be hard pressed to argue the merits of retaining what had become a patchwork of styles and discomforts.

Given the burgeoning industry that sport was evolving into, the Twickenham of old would, in a very short space of time, have truly found itself embarrassed. Ten thousand seats were available in the lower tier in time for the England v Romania game on 12th November 1994 as well as committee and Royal Box seating. The players' dressing rooms were also completed to avoid providing unnecessary temporary structures.

Phase Two was completed a year later, groaning with committee and players' facilities, senior home and away and four other dressing rooms, each with an integral warm-up area. Complete with a full medical centre with X-ray and operating facilities and a dental suite, which alone cost £1.4 million, also included were interview and press conference areas and a national fitness centre. Weights and conditioning areas competed with a bar for former international players, while on the first floor was the Spirit of Rugby restaurant and above that the RFU President's Suite and retiring room leading to the Royal Box.

As the last component of the 75,000 all-seater 'concrete horseshoe' was completed well within the timescale laid down by Taylor, the West Stand went fully operational on 18th November 1995 for the England v South Africa match before a full house. The Duke of Edinburgh formally opened by far the most complex of the three new stands on 16th December 1995 prior to a sizeable win against Western Samoa.

Although 'mostly complimentary', the RFU's minutes record 'a high degree of comment' from spectators relating to the basic seating and infrastructure. A nearby road accident after the match blocked the car park exits for several hours, and the customary conviviality of the west car park was muted due to the number of unattended committee vehicles parked adjacent to the new West Gate. The public address system, which for years had been in dire need of upgrading or renewal, remained so. Despite it working better than it had ever done, due to the employment of a professional operator, spectators remained unimpressed.

Potential television interference was one of the few concerns expressed by local residents. After the construction of the North Stand this had become a planning requirement and, having dispensed with the Union's somewhat bizarre idea of issuing replacement aerials to local residents, Husband and Co looked to BBC engineers for a solution, which eventually came in the form of signal boosters positioned on the top of the stand. Less easily assuaged was the woman who requested the planting of a screen of trees to hide from her view 'the hideous West Stand'. From the RFU's perspective, the decision three years earlier to capitalise on the available expertise, low interest rates and construction costs to finish the concrete horseshoe was a wise one.

Chapter Fifteen

A MECCA FOR DEL BOYS

The last quarter of the 20th century had its fair share of remarkable events. In Poland an electrician led the way to the first free elections in a communist country. A secular Saddam Hussein became military dictator of Iraq, and in Britain Mrs Thatcher, as leader of the Conservative Party, became not only the first woman leader of a western democracy, but changed the face of the country forever. Spectator sport in all its forms presented huge business opportunities to media tycoons such as Rupert Murdoch and the shrewder clubs such as Manchester United. At Twickenham, where once old stands rotted and crumbled while the RFU built suites of offices or pontificated about parking, vestiges of this mindset survived towards a new millennium.

The 1995-6 season augured well for the future with England again becoming the Five Nations Champions. But now England Rugby needed to shift its strength in the northern hemisphere towards beating the likes of South Africa. Despite the introduction of a Rugby World Cup, the Five Nations still occupied the premier slot in the rugby calendar and continued to attract sell-out crowds. Much to their chagrin, New Zealand, Australia and South Africa continued to play the better rugby but to much smaller crowds, hence the invention of the Tri-Nations tournament.

Back home, the core politic of the game was also irrevocably altered.

On 26th August 1995, almost 100 years to the day since the rugby game split in two, the International Rugby Board declared Rugby Union an 'open' game with no prohibition on payment or the provision of other material benefit to any person involved in the game. The old regime was dismantled and the door was finally opened to the much-dreaded spectre of professionalism. With large borrowings, the RFU was hardly in a position to fight measures designed to keep the rugby game alive and to keep HQ afloat.

During a search for extra cash England were almost expelled from the Five Nations for striking up a separate agreement with a satellite television company. With packages worth in the region of £300 million signed between the southern hemisphere and Rupert Murdoch's News Corporation, the floodgates were now well and truly open to full-on commercial exploitation.

If the soul of Twickenham was said to have packed the old South Terrace, then that same spirit survived in different ways as one by one greater and loftier neighbours embraced the pitch to form a great concrete horseshoe. The Union had spent some £70 million over the previous seven years on the redevelopment of Twickenham, leading *Rugby World* magazine to praise the RFU for having the courage against the backdrop of the worst economic recession for half a century 'to undertake one of the largest rebuilding programmes in modern-day sport'.

Around £34 million was owed to the bank, but under Union rules, borrowing capacity was £50 million, which left a considerable available balance. The shell of the West Stand came in under £16 million and demand for tickets stood at five times the supply, so it made no sense for the masterplan to grind to a halt at this stage and leave the concrete doughnut uncompleted.

Looking down from the top row of the North Stand, with the field of play laid out like some massive, live-action board game, the aspect beyond ended in an odd chasm formed through the jaws of the East and West Stands, half occupied by what was now the oldest part of the complex; a gateway that had stood sentinel to the 21st century for less than a decade, but which had become little more than a cat flap trying to do the job of a garage door.

In some respects a touch of William Cail's cavalier spirit would not have gone amiss in an organisation that had become bogged down by central control of committees, budgets and expenditure. Despite the buoyancy of the sporting marketplace, Twickenham at the dawn of the new millennium was losing around £10 million a year. Beyond the odd fair or event, fresh opportunities to generate big money were stymied by a near-schizoid approach to management.

Huge amounts of time and effort were expended on matters of minor importance, such as the use of large sun umbrellas in the west car park. Car parks were deemed essentially for parking cars and not for picnics, which caused such an uproar that umbrellas up to garden size were declared fine, provided they were erected at the front or rear of cars only and not at the sides.

This puzzling ambiguity of purpose was picked up by *Rugby World*, which tried to balance the RFU's trepidation in the prevailing economic climate against the game's extraordinary explosion. Not that Twickenham was failing completely as the RFU's principal asset. Debentures served their purpose, but they were nothing more than a series of loans waiting to be repaid.

Ticket sales aside, a healthy stream of revenue starting to come on line from Twickenham Experience Ltd ensured that cash flowed through tills in shops, restaurants and bars seven days a week; money that could be spent on projects such as the repositioning of the Rowland Hill Memorial to form a triumphal entrance leading from the west car park, crowned with the ground's freshly gilded 'Coates Lion'. The product of a highly successful 19th-century reconstituted stone process, the beast first made its appearance at Twickenham in 1971 as a gift from the Greater London Council to mark the Union's centenary celebrations.

One story has it that Twickenham's lion was originally one of a pair that graced the entrance to Waterloo Station. Another says that it stood opposite the Houses of Parliament on Westminster Bridge, and yet another that it formerly belonged to the Lion Brewery on the South Bank of the Thames. As to its exact origins, the last investigation found that it was discovered languishing in a GLC storage yard.

On its arrival at Twickenham, Harold Clark was instructed to fix the gift on top of the Rowland Hill Gate. Against his better judgement, the Ground Committee insisted that the creature faced into the stadium, where 'the public would be looking up the lion's backside as they entered the ground'. This, so it is said, was for the benefit of the Welsh who were at the time more of a force to be reckoned with. Unveiled on 29th April 1972 at a cost of £393 to prepare, restore, paint, transport and erect, the statue was removed during the construction of the new West Stand, cleaned, gilded and resited to the tune of £100,000.

The newly positioned Rowland Hill Memorial also received the addition of two life-sized bronze statues by world-renowned sculptor Gerald Laing and a plaque in memory of Peter Bromage, the Honorary Treasurer under whose financial guidance the funding for the East and West Stands was put in place.

After 11th April 1999, the Five Nations was no more. The four home nations and France were joined by Italy to create the Six Nations championship. Born before the First World War in the days of Empire, legend has it that it was the French press who coined the Five Nations tag (*Tournoi des Cinq Nations*) in the 1920s. The oldest championship on the Rugby Union calendar was remarkable in as much as it was not until 1993 that the first trophy was presented and with it a proper set of laws laid down. Prior to that, custom and practice had reigned supreme, with the rules of engagement mostly established by commentators on the game, rather than its administrators.

Moving closer towards the new millennium, England, having beaten Australia for the first time in 12 years, had arrived at the top table of international rugby in their fourth successive victory against southern hemisphere opposition. They beat South Africa 25-17 before a capacity crowd of 75,000 and triumphed over France on home turf and then Scotland and Italy in a relentless pursuit of a Six Nations Grand Slam. The England team went on to again beat Australia 21-15 for the Cook Cup, thrash a hapless Romania 134-0 and crush the Springboks 29-9.

The staging of the Lincoln Financial Group Rugby League World Cup in 2000, the 2001 Silk Cup Challenge Cup, the Zurich Premiership Final as well as more England internationals created the most acceptable opportunities for Twickenham to do what it does best. But with every conceivable commercial and marketing endeavour fully exploited, diversification other than the playing of more games each season appeared to be the only feasible option for increasing revenue. The once formidable Wembley was spent and its days numbered. It was open season for other London venue operators such as the RFU.

Following discussions with the government, the British Olympic Association and UK Athletics, the Union carried out a feasibility study. It was confirmed that the stadium might well stage the 2005 World Athletics Championships and possibly host the 2012 Olympic Games – subject to a number of considerations, not least of which was the ubiquitous problem of maximizing accommodation. In reporting their new agenda to the wider community, the RFU claimed heroically that when approached by the government to do what it could for British sport, there was a duty to help.

There were however a number of issues involving or affecting Richmond and Hounslow boroughs, the various transport authorities to improve existing road and rail links, and policing implications. Then there were the concerns of local residents and their elected representatives worried by plans to transform Twickenham into a multi-purpose operation, not only capable of staging athletic and other major sporting championships, but also large-scale musical events.

At a public meeting held in February 2000, residents from Twickenham, Hounslow and Isleworth protested that while an expanded operation at Twickenham might bring about prestige and employment, the general feeling was that the area was not appropriate for such a venue. One resident envisaged Twickenham station becoming 'something approaching the size of

Waterloo'. Another feared the transformation of this 'historical village into an Olympic village', although the location of this rural idyll remained a mystery, as did its 'village green doomed to make way for a warm-up area'. Less hysterically, it was pointed out that there were no hotels in the immediate area and all the banks, restaurants and other core services were mostly in Richmond.

Inside the stadium, the focus of attention was on the South Stand, sitting uncomfortably as it did like a loose tooth awaiting extraction. Never more than a compromise brought about by the conditions of the Safety of Sports Grounds Act, in the new vision for Twickenham the days were numbered for this poor relation lurking at its southern end.

On 24th March 2000, UK Athletics, Sport England, Government Office London and British Olympics met to review likely venues for the World Athletics Championships. Twickenham failed to make the shortlist because of local opposition and the logistics of a Twickenham tube extension. Lea Valley in Enfield was chosen instead, a decision welcomed by Twickenham residents and councillors who claimed that the town would not have been able to cope. The Conservative councillor and Greater London Assembly candidate Tony Arbour was pleased as the transport links were so poor and patently unable to cope with such an influx.

The leader of Richmond Council, Sir David Williams, was never optimistic about Twickenham's chances and was 'almost completely convinced' that the stadium's chances as a possible venue for the World Athletics Championships was 'off the agenda'. Going on informal comments made by the RFU, he got the impression that they had little real hope themselves. The President of the Richmond Chamber of Commerce, however, was disappointed that a unique opportunity for businesses in the borough and a chance 'to enhance life for residents' had been missed. It was felt that another opportunity would present itself and when it did it should be grabbed.

Like its home ground, the England game had also moved on apace. 'Awesome England' now occupied the summit of the Zurich world rankings above New Zealand. It cut deep swathes through Six Nations opposition to clinch the Triple Crown for the 22nd time. That the game had moved on would be an understatement; so too at HQ where, until the marketing ethic was fully embraced, the RFU was something of an innocent abroad.

To its credit, the Union hierarchy was ever mindful not to lose sight of its core aims and objectives. It was sensitive not to encourage any 'perceived change of atmosphere and character that may attend Twickenham in its wake'. If HQ was to enter the age of commercialism then its custodians recognised that as 'the tweed and cloth image' generally gave way to 'the grey flannels and blazer', they had to 'resist the dubious virtues of turning the place into a Mecca for "Del Boys"'. But now the days of the blazer and grey flannels were over and it was time for the Armani and the Gucci suits to take over.

Chapter Sixteen

PAST POLITICS, PRESENT HISTORY

Just as earlier Union stalwarts William Cail and Charles Marriott eventually succumbed to 'a new period of development at Twickenham', so 75 years later their successors were the focus of a radical regime change. A Chief Executive of the Rugby Football Union was appointed, the financial decline was arrested and a slimmed-down Union hierarchy was setting about the 'Masterplan for Twickenham'. On 10th September 2002, the RFU formally announced what had been common knowledge for the past year and more.

At a projected cost of around £80 million, the vision was by October 2004 to raise the all-seater capacity of the ground from 75,000 to 82,000 with the rebuilding of the South Stand. As part of a whole new complex, conference and exhibition space would be included, as well as a health and fitness club, a 400-seater performing arts venue for use by local music and drama groups, and as many as 200 new jobs to help assuage any local dissent. Into the equation was recycled the idea of incorporating a hotel into a new South Stand. Of the six VIP suites overlooking the playing area, however, prospective guests were minded by one wag in a letter to the *Richmond and Twickenham Times* to the close proximity to that harbour of ordure, the Mogden Sewerage Works.

Funding the new build would be realised through a

mixture of reduced dependency on television income, loans, debentures and commercial debt. The possibility of a grant from the National Lottery would supersede the Union's remaining £19 million bank loan due for repayment in August 2003.

With an extra 7,000 seats in the new South Stand by 2005, plus all the fresh streams of revenue coming on line a year later, the RFU's Chief Executive was 'entirely comfortable' about the ability to fund the project. Immortal words within the context of a Twickenham history littered with such assurances, mostly consigned to tears before bedtime.

Subject to planning permission being granted by the London Borough of Richmond upon Thames, it was hoped that work would start in June 2003, with the new South Stand completed by October 2004. This suited the rugby calendar well with a perfect window of opportunity provided by the World Cup to be held in Australia. The commercial facilities would open a year later, exactly one hundred years after William Cail was inspired to create a home and headquarters for England Rugby and the Rugby Football Union.

Mark Souster in *The Times* imagined that the RFU would enjoy a more favourable reception from the recently elected Conservative authority as opposed to its Liberal Democrat predecessor. However, the new leader of Richmond upon Thames Council and the Greater London Authority representative for the Borough of Hounslow was one and the same, and general support for the scheme was mixed. Hounslow councillors were prepared to wait and see exactly what effect the scheme was likely to have, whereas the leader of Richmond council remained specifically ambiguous. 'Most of the time we are proud of the RFU,' he said, 'but on match days it can be a different story. The stadium is a blessing and a curse.' Whereas the Union envisaged 'minimal' impact on the local community resulting from its latest scheme, it clearly had a good deal of convincing to do.

One of remarkably few letters on the subject printed in the *Richmond and Twickenham Times* took a pop at local authority officials and elected members with regard to the loss of the borough's world famous icerink, which was sold to developers in 1991 on the hollow promise of a replacement facility. The council should have made more of an effort to work with the RFU than against it, was the view of this correspondent. That done, then 'we would be reading of a redeveloped stand with an underground ice rink in the foundations, rather than the vague "community use" facilities outlined'.

Sir David Williams, the former leader of Richmond Council, expressed his concern that the Rugby Football Union 'was continuing to evolve into an aggressive commercial entity and not fitting into what they were meant to stand for, and that is a national representative for amateur sport'. The RFU might have spent time explaining its changed remit since 1995, but instead chose to point to a potential boost in the local economy in the region of £40 million per year. Gone were the days of solid, deeply rooted RFU men bumbling along with little appetite for turning Twickenham into something called a 'total event experience'.

It was the first visit of New Zealand in 1905 that had fired William Cail's inspiration. Back then England was barely able to compete and so beating the All Blacks before a capacity crowd at Twickenham has always been something special. With mission accomplished in a spellbinding 31-28 win in November 2002, this was followed by victory over Australia two weeks later

transport, access and safety measures in the stadium area, covering the likes of CCTV cameras, cycle routes, pedestrian crossings, signage, parking enforcement and publicity covering all transport and travel related to events at Twickenham.

A significant investment had already been made in shuttle buses to and from Richmond, resulting in an increase from 1,500 to 9,000 using the free service. Also, with the South Stand used as a backdrop to the Stones' concert, the numbers attending would be a third less than at international matches. Despite this, letters began to appear in the local papers denouncing the RFU as a 'neighbour from hell'. One correspondent claimed that the goalposts had been shifted with regard to the agreed fixture list with all the resultant negative impact on the local community. Tesco had already 'sold their soul to the devil' and the council was behaving like 'a rabbit dazzled by headlights' in the face of the RFU's aggressive development.

Twickenham Stadium, so another critic concluded, had outgrown its environment and should move on. The 'vast empty spaces between Feltham and Ashford' was suggested, with no immediate housing to create a living hell for residents, and where the RFU could even have its own railway station. The South Stand was viewed as by no means the last major development for the 'omnipresent entertainment centre', with the horror spreading towards the open plains of Kneller Hall, once more flirting with the threat of redundancy.

Some residents of Eel Pie Island feared a fan pilgrimage to the site of the Stones' birthplace could lead to the island's bridge collapsing into the Thames. Celebrity islander and inventor of the clockwork radio Trevor Baylis wound himself up at the prospect of one word from Mick Jagger and the island being overrun with pilgrims. The inventor's idea for a cage to protect the islanders and their bridge was not taken up, nor indeed was it required as rock 'n' roll history was made at Twickenham Rugby Ground on Sunday 24th August 2003 with responsible behaviour topping the bill.

The band was due to make its first appearance on the Saturday but Sir Mick Jagger had been struck down by a throat infection which meant a number of European dates had to be cancelled. However, an ailing Sir Mick assured the press that he would be suitably recharged for a Sunday evening kick-off 'in our home town... No one has ever played in the Twickenham Rugby Club (sic) before,' he said, 'so we're very privileged.'

Many of the disappointed local would-be revellers had to content themselves with sitting in their gardens to catch what they could of 252,000 watts of sound and to watch the stage pyrotechnics blast out of the stadium into the warm night air. In its fullest ever account of proceedings at the ground, the *Richmond and Twickenham Times* declared, 'Twickenham couldn't fail to be impressed... The Grandads of rock and roll rocked on... Satisfaction guaranteed'.

The RFU had set up a special community hotline, where officers from the council and the Union's own consultants were on hand to respond to complaints. Only six were received during the soundchecks and throughout the concert, with one resident complaining they could not hear and asking for the sound to be turned up. Eighty-six-year-old Don Parks, one of the longest serving Whitton Road residents, watched the orderly parade of fans pouring in and out of the ground from his cottage next door to where another

Billy Williams once lived. 'I suppose I ought to be flogging something,' he lamented.

In a late September letter to the leader of Richmond Council, Ken Livingstone, the Mayor of London, felt that if the South Stand scheme was to be accepted it should deliver a comprehensive package of traffic management measures and public transport improvements. Replicating almost exactly the former Greater London Council's concerns over the existing South Stand, the current setting and architectural quality of the residential development was deemed to be unsatisfactory and required reconsideration. In short, the Mayor was minded to direct refusal of planning permission unless a more satisfactory package was provided.

The former leader of the Greater London Council did, however, conclude that the development would bring benefits to the local economy and to London as whole 'through the completion of a world renowned sporting venue'. The decision was with Richmond Council, although the Mayor highlighted matters that were of mutual concern, especially the issue of infrastructure. The assumption was now that the RFU would submit an amended application dealing with this, and more comprehensively with the concerns of businesses and local residents.

London's Chamber of Commerce welcomed the £70 million redevelopment as a great investment in London and Britain's economy, although some local traders remained sceptical. Also, the key area of access remained the greatest concern. Ways were being looked at to relieve the congestion of the A316 Great Chertsey Road and to improve visitor access to and from Twickenham station. It was a travel plan that sat oddly with wider ambitions to build a London

Crossrail link. While improving services to and from the centre of London, the new link would see the closure of the District Line at Richmond and a loss of one of the few Underground stations within a forty-five-minute walk of Twickenham Rugby Ground; not that the stadium featured in the debate. Overall, the Leader of Richmond Council argued that losing the District Line at Richmond was a regressive step and not one in the best interest of the thousands who used the service daily.

In joining forces with Hounslow, it was further argued that an enhanced service for all would result if use were made of the Hounslow Loop Line, which would then include a better service for Whitton. Incredibly, almost a century had passed since these same concerns were first expressed for improved rail services, a halt for Whitton or indeed an extension of the underground system.

Whereas for the most part the RFU's input into such matters remained stoically muted as the England team flew off down under to bring back the World Cup, a transport strategy was being digested by local resident groups, councillors, council officials and amenity societies. The Union expressed interest in the Mayor's comments, but centred its interest on anxieties about the replacement of existing housing, which it felt was not insurmountable. As far as the concerns of local traders and residents were concerned, the RFU's surveys showed 59 per cent of the latter were in favour of the scheme and businesses even more so at 69 per cent.

As all eyes turned to the 2003 Rugby World Cup hosted by Australia, HQ stood dormant and the perfect window of opportunity for the RFU to implement its plans passed by. Local interest centred on Mogden

Sewerage Works, which had received yet another final warning from Hounslow Council about 'The Great Stink' and 'plagues of mosquitoes' blighting the lives of residents and spectators alike. On the global stage, interest in the England Rugby game was never keener.

The greatest sporting event of the year culminating in a nail-biting final against the home team looking for a triple win was dashed by the boot of Jonny Wilkinson in the final seconds of extra time. Like something straight from the pages of *Boy's Own* magazine, victory was secured for England and a homecoming for the coveted Webb Ellis Cup at Twickenham's Museum of Rugby.

The sterling silver and gilded cup nicknamed 'Bill' by the Australians after their second World Cup victory in 1991 was made by Crown jewellers Garrard and Co of London in 1906 – the very year that another Bill (Billy Williams) set out on his quest for an England ground. The cup remained in the firm's vaults for 81 years awaiting selection as a suitable trophy, until in 1987 it was chosen as the prize for the newly established Rugby World Cup. The William Webb Ellis Cup, to give it its proper name, was in tribute to the Rugby schoolboy who, as legend has it, picked up a football and ran with it in 1823, thereby inventing the non-dribbling derivative of soccer.

The RFU wasted no time in cashing in on the nation's reverie and again rolled out its plans for the proposed new South Stand to offer England Rugby, at last, the stadium it deserved. The benefits to the local community were intensely revisited. Speaking at a breakfast meeting with Richmond Chamber of Commerce, the Leader of the Council said he expected the huge interest generated by England Rugby's win to have positive financial spin-offs for local firms and provide a big boost for tourism and business in the area.

With Twickenham the home of England Rugby and now the home of the world champions, the council would, 'of course, encourage and support the efforts of the RFU to boost business and the profile of the borough'. The council was committed to making the borough an attractive environment for companies to operate in. A new Civic Pride strategy, geared to ensuring that the borough became an even more attractive area, went arm in arm with a vision of the district as a magnet for tourists. And, for the first time in the borough's history, as well as its Royal parks, historic palaces and world-famous gardens was included 'international sport' in the form of Twickenham Rugby Ground as part of its 'unrivalled heritage'.

The ground was now on the map internationally as never before, but domestically issues of the past outside of the planned development resurrected themselves in a near repeat performance of two decades earlier. Townscape and visual impact, transportation, noise, infrastructure, construction and services all needed to be resolved across a plethora of committees and meetings.

A large number of local residents, particularly those living along Whitton Road and therefore the most directly affected, opposed the scheme, complaining that the plans to demolish 22 houses and replace them with a hotel, fitness centre and conference centre would utterly transform their environment. Whitton Road would be changed forever by the impact of such an enormous structure. The report produced by the planning officer understated the fact that there would be a 'significant change' to the road.

In acknowledging the concerns of those living opposite the ground, the RFU pointed to the 'exceptional circumstances' in so far as it had been in residence long before its neighbours as a major presence in the area. The argument that it was therefore more difficult to object to the 'mass, design and layout' within the context of the application, attracted rebuttals from residents who claimed that this was 'unjust'. Many residents had lived in Whitton Road since the current South Stand was built in 1981, and it was reasonable to assume that it would remain for at least their lifetimes.

The report revealed that Hounslow Council was opposed to the scheme, saying it was too big for the surrounding area and no consideration had been given to local residents. As well as letters from residents' groups, Richmond Council received 66 letters of objection, mostly concerning the change of use for the area from residential to commercial use. As well as the matter of intrusion associated with the new stand there was still the building and strategic problems such as transport and the extra traffic to be resolved.

With regard to the demolition of the characterful Victorian and Edwardian villas standing in the way, there would normally have been an outcry at their proposed destruction. But there was not. Those local societies and representative interest bodies normally so vocal on such matters looked to the overall benefits accrued from the package. A letter from the Twickenham Society was among a further 76 received in support of the scheme. Looking to the new 400-seat community arts space, the Richmond upon Thames Arts Council and Thames Performing Arts Festival, the Twickenham Operatic Society, the Richmond Operatic Society,

Twickenham Choral Society, Kew Wind Orchestra, The Edmundian Players, The Children's Shakespeare Company, The Joyful Company of Singers and The Eel Pie Club all gave their full support. Only the view from Richmond Hill gave rise to minor palpitations.

Overall it was generally felt that the new build would not have a significant impact. It completed the oval to the height of the existing structure and moreover the use of tinted glass would reduce light reflection to make the ground a less obvious blight on the landscape. Under the planning officer's recommendation, if permission was granted it would also include an agreement by which the RFU would have to put even more into the pot to serve those members of the wider community without interests in the arts or rugby. A sum of £1.4 million was recommended by way of an example to pay for increased public transport, town centre improvements and other initiatives to meet the extra activity.

But it was the scale of the plan that most vexed the residents of Whitton Road, who looked to 'a massive loss of privacy' with guests from the hotel across the road able to peer directly into their homes. The Chairman of the Residents' Association explained that members knew when they moved in that they were living opposite a rugby ground, but they did not realise that it would one day become 'Blackpool illuminations with a hotel'. He added that because of the ground's sheer size it would be like living opposite a skyscraper. In defence, the RFU's architect believed that the scheme humanised the complex and gave it 'a face', rather than a harsh, exposed concrete skeleton.

The aim of the new stand was not only to complete the job, but to reduce the physical impact of the whole development along Whitton Road by setting it back so as to avoid direct confrontation with houses on the south side of the road. Trees would be planted along the terraces of the upper storeys to secure privacy from hotel guests tempted to look into the lives of people living opposite. Sufficient to dispirit any architect, the design was considered 'interesting'. Its nature was considered to be 'relatively subdued', with little erosion of amenity to the wider area.

During a gruelling four-hour planning meeting, where councillors weighed up the concerns of the ground's immediate neighbours with the potential benefits to the borough as a whole, it was the traffic consultant who received a particularly thorough grilling from the committee on his predictions following the development. But community leaders, warmed by the prospect of attracting new jobs to the area as well as other major economic spin-offs, largely welcomed the announcement, and gave the scheme their unanimous approval.

Subject to endorsement from the Government Office for London and the Mayor of London, the Victorian and Edwardian villas were to be cleared and replaced with a new South Stand complex, boosting the stadium's capacity by 7,500 to 82,000 and accommodating a 200-bedroom hotel, health and leisure club, conference and exhibition centre, basement parking, new ticket sales facilities, shop and offices, and the community arts facility. The pair of cottages nestling at the tip of the North Car Park would make way for two blocks of 'affordable' flats to complete the £70 million project.

The leader of Richmond Council, Councillor Tony Arbour, enthused over an exciting scheme of national and international importance, pronouncing the stadium as 'the home of English rugby, a showpiece ground which focuses the eyes of the rugby world.

The redevelopment will ensure it becomes truly fit for the world champions'. Not only had the England team won the Rugby World Cup for their country, but arguably aided greatly the victory on their home turf.

At a special meeting of the Council, a motion was passed to grant the freedom of the Borough of Richmond upon Thames to local heroes, Lawrence Dallaglio and Joe Worsley, of London Wasps, and NEC Harlequins' Jason Leonard and Will Greenwood. However, in proposing the motion and praising the achievement of the England rugby team in the World Cup, the council leader shifted the home of English Rugby out of Twickenham and into Richmond.

With the buzz still evident weeks after the historic victory, an overwhelming majority of people asked by a local paper if they thought it was a good idea to expand Twickenham agreed that it was. More things coming to the area would mean better business, especially on rugby days. One rugby fan thought it made sense to complete the stadium, but expressed reservations about the loss of what few houses of architectural and historic interest remained in that part of the borough. Their removal brick by brick and reassembly elsewhere would have made the scheme perfect.

Most people asked felt that as the stadium was there it should be celebrated. One resident of the borough living some distance from the ground saw no problem. People living near it, he suggested, had known for more than 50 years that a rugby stadium was there. With rugby a part of Twickenham for the best part of a century, not developing the stadium would be like moving Wembley Stadium to Cornwall. Pop concerts and football were out. Otherwise, Twickenham was rugby; the stadium had put the place on the map. It was what Twickenham was famous for.

As well as having major economic spin-offs for west London, providing a massive boost for employment and the economy of the region as a whole, Twickenham town centre's manager added that the project was the logical completion and evolution of Twickenham's greatest and most well-known public asset and would bring more people into the town. Coupled with the additional spectators on match days, the greater benefit would be from the four-star hotel, the largest in the borough, that would attract many visitors to the area and its many tourist attractions.

Not surprisingly, the RFU was delighted with the result. In the past, substantial amounts of time, effort and money had been spent improving the stadium, but it was only within the past decade that they had enjoyed unity with the local authority. And they had employed a community relations strategy designed to maintain local popular support for an even shorter period.

Chapter Seventeen

FULL CIRCLE

With the improvements made to the stadium, eyes turned to hosting the 2007 Rugby World Cup. In a letter of support from the UK government, Prime Minister Tony Blair declared that the staging of the event in England would present an 'ideal opportunity to show the sporting world our excellent facilities, the RFU's world-renowned organisational expertise and excellent hospitality'. But it was not to be. France took the honours after defeating England in a two-way bidding race by 18 votes to three, which represented a shock landslide defeat for England. Graeme Cattermole, chairman of the RFU Management Board, said following the announcement in April 2003: 'We are obviously very disappointed by the decision but the voting process has been a democratic one and we accept the outcome'.

A year later and Manchester United legend Sir Bobby Charlton visited Twickenham for the first time to announce nominations for the 2004 Laureus World Sports Awards, which included the Laureus World Team of the Year Award for the England Rugby team and Jonny Wilkinson as World Sportsman of the Year. Sir Bobby found himself most impressed with the ground and its great atmosphere. 'Twickenham would be ideal for soccer,' he proclaimed in his innocence, seeing 'big games to be staged in England instead of Cardiff while Wembley is being rebuilt.' Rumours that the Football Association was keen to use Twickenham as a temporary base for international soccer matches, including the FA Cup Final, had been circulating since May 1996. Then the Chairman of the Twickenham Society argued that Wembley was a different sort of place, not at the heart of a residential area like Twickenham. Worried residents were assured by the RFU that soccer was not an option at Twickenham as the game could not be legally played there because it was not segregated. Two years later, however, and the RFU announced a complete U-turn following a fresh proposal from the FA. Deeply unimpressed, Richmond Council's assertion that it did not approve of football coming to Twickenham was seen by the RFU as a 'blow to community relations'. They urged people to write in and state their views, which they did.

'The RFU is tempted by the financial benefits afforded by the deal,' spotted one shrewd complainant. 'With so much money involved, the RFU had no regard for the local area,' decided another. Eight years later, despite Sir Bobby's heretical remarks making their way onto the sports pages of the *Richmond and Twickenham Times*, not a single rant made its way to the letters editor. In looking to build a new South Stand, however, involving the mass demolition of antique houses that had for decades stymied the stadium's development, attention was now focused on the ramifications of the scheme on the residents living along the opposite side of Whitton Road. History, with a degree of inevitability as far as Twickenham is concerned, was about to repeat itself. It was in January 1967 that the RFU sent a letter to the Minister of Housing and Local Government requesting that their planning application for a South Stand be reconsidered. All the necessary approaches had been made to the householders flanking the southern perimeter of the stadium. Indeed, so eager had been the Union to push on with its plan that it had instructed its solicitors to accept the 'inflated asking prices' for as many of the houses as were available. By August, the remaining properties were purchased and a further application for planning was lodged for work to begin in April 1968 for completion in August 1970. Permission was granted the same day that the six houses in question were vacated and the entire scheme had to be abandoned due to a massive underestimation of the costs.

Ten years later and the severe deterioration of the South Terrace forced a second planning application to be submitted, which faltered on the back of numerous finance packages being refused by either one of the two local authorities sharing control over the Twickenham site. Only the idea of a hotel incorporated into the new stand complex found favour with both Richmond and Hounslow Councils, but sadly attracted no interest from the various brewery groups and hotel chains approached. But the RFU had no option other than to proceed, which it did by way of a compromise stand that lasted only twenty years before the Union found itself again looking to provide a more companionable addition to the south end of its stadium. Inevitably, the decision resulted in a fresh tangle with the neighbours.

On this occasion it was the residents living on the south side of Whitton Road complaining that not only would they for the first time find themselves fully exposed to the ground, but to a new, expanded development, described by one correspondent to *The Hounslow Informer* as being of Blackpool Illuminations proportions. Homeowners asked if there was anything that could be done in planning conditions that might alleviate the impact of the proposed blight on their lives. The MP for Twickenham, Vincent Cable, observed that the council's decision was a difficult one, based as it was on the wider perspective, but with the need to balance the very real worries and objections of a minority. In a letter to the Chief Executive of the RFU, Dr Cable hoped that the Union would follow through an offer of compensation by buying up homes potentially seriously depreciated in value. Planning law, he added, was defective in not allowing for such compensation, but he hoped in this case that the RFU would be magnanimous.

Financially, the aftermath of the Rugby World Cup anticipated a draining of the RFU's coffers to the tune of £9 million in annual revenue and a bottom-line loss of around £6 million. The series marked the base of a four-year financial cycle for the northern hemisphere game. Scotland reported losses of £8.6 million and Ireland €6.3 million. But the surge of interest in the game in England since the trophy was lifted had led to a boom in the RFU's merchandise sales, which were twice as high as predicted, with hospitality income also exceeding expectations. The Union's debt-free position with net cash assets of £30 million was key to underpinning the redevelopment of the new South Stand, so another round of recompense was about as welcome to the RFU as a warm wind wafting over the arena from a ripe Mogden on a match day.

Taking on board some of the concerns expressed during the consultation process, new designs for the South Stand redevelopment were released. It was to be smaller in scale than the original scheme and include a reduction in height, 44 fewer rooms in the hotel with 50 per cent less facing directly onto Whitton Road. The total floor space of the development was reduced by 16 per cent and the basement car park scrapped to minimise road traffic activity. Still included was the all-important package of local community benefits designed to appease the concerns of residents highlighted during the planning process. As well as the £400,000 performing arts centre, the number of tickets available to local residents on England match days would be increased and the £2.5 million contribution to Richmond Council as agreed in the conditions of the planning permission would be used to improve public transport, CCTV and general improvements to Twickenham town centre. Improvement of match day routes to the stadium and Twickenham station, the ubiquitous affordable housing and landscaping also remained. On the field of play, however, the motivational aspect of the RFU's prime ambassadors was losing something of its sparkle.

The Six Nations saw a lacklustre England missing an injured Jonny Wilkinson and newly retired World Cup-winning captain Martin Johnson finally relinquish Fortress Twickenham to a revitalised Ireland. The bastion was almost lost again to a rejuvenated Wales, and failing to beat France in Paris was only a precursor to some bad times ahead in the southern hemisphere. England captain Lawrence Dallaglio insisted that there was no need to panic and that his side could bounce back from the hat-trick of defeats including, after two Test losses in New Zealand, a 51-15 mauling at the hands of Australia in Brisbane – England's worst defeat in six years. But the newly knighted Head Coach Sir Clive Woodward was optimistic. England would emerge all the stronger when they faced Australia, South Africa and Canada at Twickenham, he maintained.

Of the victorious England squad involved on that momentous night in Sydney when Martin Johnson lifted the World Cup, only nine were still part of it when the 2004 autumn internationals began, and only four of the fifteen that started at the Telstra Stadium were still in situ, with hooker Steve Thompson the only survivor from England's triumphant pack. While Matt Dawson's media career saw him unceremoniously axed, Will Greenwood, Ben Kay and Ben Cohen each strived to reclaim their status. With Richard Hill joining Jonny Wilkinson on the injury list, the way was clear for Jason Robinson to lead England into what was hoped would be a new era. Looking ahead, meanwhile, to do for the game of dribblers what he had done for the passing game, Sir Clive focused his attention on the 2005 British and Irish Lions tour to New Zealand, leaving Andy Robinson, his replacement as England Head Coach, to name an unchanged side to play Australia in the Investec Challenge autumn internationals at Twickenham following England's outstanding 32-16 win over Tri-Nations champions South Africa.

The green light was given for the new £80 million stand at Twickenham on Thursday 2nd December 2004 when Richmond Council's planning committee unanimously approved the Rugby Football Union's revised application for planning permission. For what were described by the RFU as commercial and operational reasons, its decision to amend the original scheme to one more likely to find greater favour from all interest groups had paid dividends. Smaller in scale than the previous scheme, the core proposal to fully enclose and surround the playing area and increase capacity from the current 75,000 to 82,000 remained. Sponsors' names now attached to various elements of the development. The 156-bed four-star Marriott hotel still included six VIP suites with views over the pitch. A Virgin Active health and fitness club and a new Rugby Store would join the conference and exhibition space and the 400-seat performing arts centre. Demolition of the existing stand was set for June 2005, prior to commencement of the piling works programmed for August, with the lower tier of seating due for completion by the start of the 2005-6 season. When completed in time for the 2006 autumn internationals, 'English Rugby would at last get the national stadium it deserved,' declared stadium director, Richard Knight, 'complete with tangible benefits for the local community.'

Twenty-five years had passed since a nervous Rugby Football Union agreed to a low-key start by tentatively placing its feet on the first rungs of the corporate hospitality ladder. The four tents pitched on the front lawn, then realizing £2,500, opened the door for other untapped streams of revenue long enjoyed for decades at other major and minor grounds across the globe. In its annual report for 2004, the RFU reported more than 14,000 corporate packages, including hospitality and catering revenues of over £17 million. Merchandising accounted for another £10 million and sponsorship a further £11 million. Sophisticated sectional buildings had replaced the tents to create a host of small towns stretching from the grounds of Kneller Hall and Chase Bridge School, across the west car park to east of Rugby Road on land three times rejected by the Rugby Football Union. Queues for tickets to see U2's Vertigo Tour stretched half a mile as fans waited for up to seven hours.

Despite a Welsh victory at the Millennium Stadium denying England the chance of a Six Nations Grand Slam, not a single seat remained empty at HQ on Sunday 13th February 2005 when an uninspiring

French side took full advantage of an ill-disciplined England performance in an 18-17 win over the world champions. Sliding down the world rankings, scrabbling around at the bottom of the Six Nations table without a point, and condemned to a third consecutive defeat by an Ireland on course for their first Grand Slam since 1948, England were only just ahead of Italy on points difference in the championship table and looking to beat them and Scotland to avoid clinching the wooden spoon.

When Wales beat Ireland for the first time at home in 22 years to win their first Grand Slam in 27 years, the Triple Crown and their first Six Nations championship, England ran in seven tries against Scotland to finish a frustrating Six Nations campaign. Reclaiming the Calcutta Cup and avoiding fifth place in the standings, it was an entertaining finale to the last England game to be played before spectators seated in the doomed platform at the south end of the ground. In an explosive operation exclusively revealed by the *Richmond and Twickenham Times* as presenting a possible 'terrifying hazard', the paper's source, an unnamed 'concerned demolition expert', feared that due to its post-tension design, the stand required dismantling rather than being taken down with explosives. With the ends of the support posts protected with concrete and the metal beams tensioned like elastic bands, he explained, the strain would have to be accommodated somewhere in the event of a sudden break. 'The bars might shoot out of the ends of the beams like bullets and fly for miles,' he added for good measure.

Fortunately, a spokesman for the Controlled Demolition Group, the company awarded the tender for the first stage of the £80 million project, was able to assure readers that this method of demolition was the safest and quickest option and one that would cause the least disruption to local people. The RFU confirmed that the chosen contractor was a world-leading specialist with more than 120 years of collective experience in demolishing high-rise structures. Explosive demolition was a precision science increasingly the first choice for companies and local authorities. Included in its numerous benefits over traditional demolition techniques was the safety of workers able to bring confined structures down from a distance with minimal noise and dust disruption for the public at large. Instead of taking weeks, such a process took place in a matter of seconds, reducing disturbance caused by any necessary road closures and diversions.

The reaction of locals to all of this was muted, unlike those witnesses to the demolition of Harlequins, out to beat high-flying Sale in the final game of the season to avoid relegation from the Zurich Premiership. Harlequins, once Rugby Union's pre-eminent club, enlisted by William Cail as part of his original Twickenham package, saw the unthinkable become reality on 30th April 2005. One of the oldest clubs in world rugby, and the only surviving London-based side in the Premiership, went down to Sale by just one point and was condemned to life outside of the rugby elite for the first time in a 139-year history. Days after Martin Johnson signed off at Twickenham before a 42,000 strong crowd in a hard-won victory against a mighty Jonah Lomu XV, the first mechanical digger was busy clearing another part of the ground's history, South View's once sacrosanct garden. Purchased by the RFU 80 years previously at the suggestion of William Cail as a fitting residence for the serving Secretary, the leafy retreat that once perfectly captured the civilising influence of the passing game had finally given way to 'improvement'. In the course of a few short hours it was gone.

A week later and the bulldozers had surged eastwards to level the gardens of the five other venerable villas immediately flanking the stadium's southern border. All were then secured within a wall of frail metal shutters to await the salvagers' systematic stripping them of their architectural treasures. External to the existing South Stand, the planned requirement would be to eventually demolish all 16 properties and the RFU's office block built in the late 1970s. As well as a significant amount of materials recycled from the houses, the major items of value from the stand would be the steel recycled to scrapyards and the concrete, which would be crushed and used for the new construction works. In total, it was planned to recover some 27,365 tonnes of demolition material. Once the whole area was cleared, the foundations would be removed to a depth of 1.5 metres and then backfilled with some 17,000 tonnes of recycled concrete aggregrate crushed on site and mixed with a geotextile layer to provide a firm stratum for the new construction works. The re-use of the concrete on the scheme would also greatly reduce the impact on the surrounding environment by reducing major lorry movements and the cost of the groundworks package. But not everyone was convinced as to the wisdom of operation 'Blowdown', the catchy pseudonym attaching the structure's demolition day.

Vincent Cable told the *Richmond and Twickenham Times* that some of the stadium's neighbours had expressed fears about dust settlement, accidental damage and the siting of the concrete crushing plant close to their homes. Although the Twickenham MP had no doubts himself as to the expertise employed by the RFU in ensuring a safe and controlled explosion, some of his constituents remained nervous and wanted to be absolutely clear as to who would be responsible for any unforeseen costs. In response, the RFU hand-delivered a letter to the 120 homes in the exclusion zone, detailing a full schedule of the half-day event together with an assurance that the area would be cleaned if necessary after the 'blowdown'. Not all of the local residents living in the designated exclusion zone were keen on being evacuated from their homes, but many of those who were offered hospitality and the opportunity to watch the drama from the North Stand did so.

The miserable weather blighting most of July had passed by Sunday 10th. With no wind the conditions were perfect. By 11 am an area ten times the size of the stadium complex was closed off to road and pedestrian traffic. Half an hour later and the arena was itself sealed from the outside world. The corporate boxes in the North Stand and a few rows of seating below reserved for local residents were at the same time buzzing with excitement as mindful of the flags around the stadium positioned at half-mast, marking the tragic events of the previous Thursday when innocent London commuters became the target of terrorist bombing. Serious consideration had been given to postponing the demolition as a further mark of respect, but after considerable discussions with the police and with the plans at such an advanced stage, it was decided that the operation should continue. However, all planned arrangements for media activity were cancelled and prior to the demolition, RFU President Elect, LeRoy Angel, delivered a short eulogy during which he called for one minute's silence.

The eerie wail of a wartime siren echoed about the stadium, lasting a full five minutes. Shortly afterwards, and taking most of the crowd by surprise, a warning maroon soared into the air signalling the last few seconds of the pathetic-looking stand stripped bare of all but its structural content and already separated from its two wings by traditional demolition techniques. Just weeks before, 110,000 fans of Irish rockers U2 had packed the ground for a last show of any description with the hapless stand as a backdrop. Now fewer than 1,000 heard the low crack, followed seconds later by a dull thud as 5,000 tonnes of concrete and steel came crashing down and taking most of the spectators by surprise. Those inside the ground felt very little, whereas those outside lining the A316 experienced the full blast of the detonation set to the rear of the stand and felt the ground shake. The cloud of white dust threatening to engulf the stadium reached as far as the half way line before imploding back into itself towards the mass of debris neatly piled exactly where it was planned to be. Within minutes the fine haze had cleared, revealing for the first time in two decades and (probably) for the last time in many more to come, an uninterrupted panorama of the Surrey countryside as far as the South Downs.

With the clock ticking closer towards 2009 and the centenary of the first ever game played at the RFU's ground, it can only be imagined what Messrs Cail and Williams might have thought were they able to look down on the old cabbage patch from the comfort of a hospitality box. Both men had watched that same slab of earth grow from two wooden sheds flanking a waterlogged field. Less than twenty years later, the renowned stadium engineer, Archibald Leitch, would plant one of his signature gems at the north end facing the massive concrete raft where the true spirit of Twickenham was nurtured. With the great ironclad double-decker barns later planted east and west, the Cathedral of Rugby came of age. When William Cail lit the fuse in 1905 that eventually ignited England rugby success, he might have failed to secure the best of sites in Twickenham, but his legacy has endured and prospered. In doffing an England cap to the history of the ground the President Elect in his acclamation paid tribute to Billy Williams and the seed he set for a little over five thousand pounds. In its continuing evolution as a major player on the international sporting scene, Williams and Cail would have shared a wry smile, sure in the knowledge that as their ground came full circle, and for as long as the rugby game was played there, so present history would indubitably echo past politics.

Sources and Bibliography

Archival

Public Record Office: Finance (1909–10) Act. O.S. IR 121/18/32 (field book IR 58/70092: 6996 including 6997). Edwin Coe Solicitors: Deeds of Conveyance (various 1907). Richmond upon Thames Local Studies Collection: Twickenham Local Board Minutes 1891-1895; Twickenham Urban District Council Minutes 1895-1930; Census Records 1881, 1891, 1901; Richmond Times Directory Almanac 1891; *Richmond and Twickenham Times* Almanac 1881/1888; Directories for Twickenham and Whitton 1860-1882; Kelly's Middlesex Directory 1882; Kelly's Directory of Richmond, Kew etc. 1902/1903/1907; Twickenham Rate and Parish Books (1895); Twickenham Register of Electors 1907-1909; Auction catalogue: Kneller Hall Estate 1841. Whitton Park Estate sales catalogue 1910. Metropolitan Archive: Auction Papers Whitton Lands 1904. Rugby Football Union Museum: RFU committee/subcommittee minute books 25th September 1902 – 28th May 1920; Plan of ground submitted to Twickenham UDC March 1907; From Holborn To Mayfair (collected Minutes of the RFU). Wembley Stadium Archive. National Army Museum. Department of Archives, Photographs, Films and Sound.

Newspapers & Periodicals

Richmond upon Thames Local Studies Collection: *Middlesex Chronicle; Richmond and Twickenham Times; Thames Valley Times; Richmond Herald*; Twickenham 1909-1959: article (publication unaccredited) by D R Gent. Rugby Football Union Museum (cuttings): *Observer; Daily Mail; Daily Mirror; Morning Post; The Times*. The British Library Newspaper Library: *The Times; Athletic News; Illustrated Sporting and Dramatic News*.

Maps

OS Northern Twickenham and Whitton 6-inch. 1867 OS 15-inch 1894-6 OS 6-inch Re-levelled 1913. OS 25-inch. 1960. Plan of the Parish of Twickenham 1846. Fairfield Estate sketchplan (1907)

Oral Accounts

Carverhill, Mrs. (1995) Whitton 1915-1995. Christie, Miss (1999) Twickenham Rugby Ground 1914-1999. Costa E (1990) Whitton

Sources and Bibliography

1895-1995. Duran J (1995) Whitton 1900-1995. King G (1992) Hounslow/Whitton 1930-1997. Tulip D (1993) Whitton 1925-. Underwood H (1992) Whitton 1901-1992. Williams B (1995) Whitton 1915-1995. Mr & Mrs Parks (2003) Whitton 1918-. Harding, Mr & Mrs (2003) Whitton 1915-.

Unpublished Papers

Clark, Harold (1995) Clerk of Works, RFU, 14th February 1964 – 3rd April 1982: Unpublished memoirs. Hardcastle A C (1987): Whitton, a Village within a Suburb (private publication). Wright, Alf.

Published Sources

Barrett, E (editor) (1991) *English Rugby - A Celebration*. Mainstream.

Bate. G E (1948) *And So Make a City Here: The Story of a Lost Heathland*. Thomasons Ltd.

Black, J and Lloyd, M (1994) *Football stadia developments and land-use policy and planning controls. Town and Planning Review* (Vol 65).

Blackledge, Paul *Rationalist Capitalist Concerns: William Cail and the Great Rugby Split of 1895. The international Journal of the History of Sport, Vol.18 (June 2001)*, pp.35-53. Frank Cass, London.

Bowker, Barry Morrison (1976) *England Rugby: A History of the National Side, 1871 -1976*. Cassell.

Brailsford, Dennis (1992) *British Sport: a social history*. Cambridge: Lutterworth.

Cain, John (1992) *The BBC: 70 Years of Broadcasting*. BBC.

Donnachie I *Landscapes, buildings and physical artifacts (1997) Sources and Methods: A Handbook*. Michael Drake and Ruth Finnegan (Eds). The Open University.

Ercaut, E J Howlett (1925) *The Richmond Football Club 1861-1925*.

Foster, P and Simpson D H. *Whitton Park and Whitton Place. Paper No.41 (1979)*.

Gent, D R *Twickenham 1909-1959. RFU 50th Anniversary Programme*. Richmond Local Studies Collection.

Hands, David (2000) *The Five Nations Story*. Tempus.

Inglis, Fred (1977) *The Name of the Game: Sport and Society*. London. Heinemann Educational.

Inglis, Simon (1991) *The Football Grounds of Great Britain*. Collins Willow.

Konya, Allan (1986) *Sports buildings – London: Architectural, C A Briefing and Design Guide*.

London Bus Magazine (1953) *Golden Jubilee Celebrations (1933-53)*. Introduction by Colin Stannard. London Transport Publications.

McWhirter, Ross and Titley V A (1970) *Centenary History of the Rugby Football Union*. Redwood Press Ltd.

Marshall, Rev F and Treswill, Leonard (1892, revised 1925) *Football – The Rugby Union Game*. Cassell & Co.

Matthews R C O, Fenstein C H, Odling-Smee J C (1987) *British Economic Growth 1856-1973*. Clarendon Press. Oxford. pp.336-7.

Maxwell, Gordon S. *Highwayman's Heath*. Thomasons Ltd. (first published 1935, 1938. New Edition [re-set] 1949).

Owen O L (1955) *The History of the Rugby Football Union*. Playfair Books.

Peters, Jim (2000) *Before The Stadium*. Fact&Fiction publications.

Reyburn, Wallace (1976) *Twickenham: The Story of a Rugby Ground*. George Allen & Unwin Ltd.

Sports Council (1981) *The Handbook of Sports and Recreational Building Design TEC – Vol 3: Outdoor Sports*. London: Architectural Press.

Tranter, N L (1998). *Sport, economy and society in Britain, 1750-1914 (1941)* Cambridge: Cambridge University Press.

Turner, Gordon and Turner, Alwyn W (1996) *The Trumpets Will Sound: The Story of the Royal Military School of Music Kneller Hall*. Papares Ltd.

Urwin, A C B (1982) *Commercial Nurseries and Market Gardens*. Borough of Twickenham History Society Paper no 50.

Urwin, A C B (1971) *Birket's Brook*. Borough of Twickenham History Society.

Van Doren, Carlton S; Priddle, George B; Lewis, John E (Eds) (1974) *Land & Leisure: Concepts and methods in outdoor recreation*. Second Edition. Methuen.

Wakelam, H B T (1954) *Harlequin Story*. Phoenix House Ltd.

Whitehand, JWR and Carr, Christine M H (1999) *Morphological periods, planning and reality: the case of England's inter-war suburbs*. Urban History, 26, 2.

Index

Index